IS ACADEMIC FREEDOM THREATENED BY CHINA'S INFLUENCE ON U.S. UNIVERSITIES?

HEARING

BEFORE THE

SUBCOMMITTEE ON AFRICA, GLOBAL HEALTH, GLOBAL HUMAN RIGHTS, AND INTERNATIONAL ORGANIZATIONS

OF THE

COMMITTEE ON FOREIGN AFFAIRS HOUSE OF REPRESENTATIVES

ONE HUNDRED THIRTEENTH CONGRESS

SECOND SESSION

DECEMBER 4, 2014

Serial No. 113–230

Printed for the use of the Committee on Foreign Affairs

Available via the World Wide Web: http://www.foreignaffairs.house.gov/ or http://www.gpo.gov/fdsys/

U.S. GOVERNMENT PRINTING OFFICE

91–663PDF   WASHINGTON : 2014

For sale by the Superintendent of Documents, U.S. Government Printing Office
Internet: bookstore.gpo.gov   Phone: toll free (866) 512–1800; DC area (202) 512–1800
Fax: (202) 512–2104   Mail: Stop IDCC, Washington, DC 20402–0001

COMMITTEE ON FOREIGN AFFAIRS

EDWARD R. ROYCE, California, *Chairman*

CHRISTOPHER H. SMITH, New Jersey
ILEANA ROS-LEHTINEN, Florida
DANA ROHRABACHER, California
STEVE CHABOT, Ohio
JOE WILSON, South Carolina
MICHAEL T. McCAUL, Texas
TED POE, Texas
MATT SALMON, Arizona
TOM MARINO, Pennsylvania
JEFF DUNCAN, South Carolina
ADAM KINZINGER, Illinois
MO BROOKS, Alabama
TOM COTTON, Arkansas
PAUL COOK, California
GEORGE HOLDING, North Carolina
RANDY K. WEBER SR., Texas
SCOTT PERRY, Pennsylvania
STEVE STOCKMAN, Texas
RON DeSANTIS, Florida
DOUG COLLINS, Georgia
MARK MEADOWS, North Carolina
TED S. YOHO, Florida
SEAN DUFFY, Wisconsin
CURT CLAWSON, Florida

ELIOT L. ENGEL, New York
ENI F.H. FALEOMAVAEGA, American
 Samoa
BRAD SHERMAN, California
GREGORY W. MEEKS, New York
ALBIO SIRES, New Jersey
GERALD E. CONNOLLY, Virginia
THEODORE E. DEUTCH, Florida
BRIAN HIGGINS, New York
KAREN BASS, California
WILLIAM KEATING, Massachusetts
DAVID CICILLINE, Rhode Island
ALAN GRAYSON, Florida
JUAN VARGAS, California
BRADLEY S. SCHNEIDER, Illinois
JOSEPH P. KENNEDY III, Massachusetts
AMI BERA, California
ALAN S. LOWENTHAL, California
GRACE MENG, New York
LOIS FRANKEL, Florida
TULSI GABBARD, Hawaii
JOAQUIN CASTRO, Texas

AMY PORTER, *Chief of Staff*   THOMAS SHEEHY, *Staff Director*
JASON STEINBAUM, *Democratic Staff Director*

SUBCOMMITTEE ON AFRICA, GLOBAL HEALTH, GLOBAL HUMAN RIGHTS, AND INTERNATIONAL ORGANIZATIONS

CHRISTOPHER H. SMITH, New Jersey, *Chairman*

TOM MARINO, Pennsylvania
RANDY K. WEBER SR., Texas
STEVE STOCKMAN, Texas
MARK MEADOWS, North Carolina

KAREN BASS, California
DAVID CICILLINE, Rhode Island
AMI BERA, California

CONTENTS

Page

WITNESSES

Perry Link, Ph.D., chancellorial chair for innovative teaching, University
    of California, Riverside 6
Thomas Cushman, Ph.D., Deffenbaugh de Hoyos Carlson chair in the social
    sciences, Wellesley College 15
Xia Yeliang, Ph.D., visiting fellow, Center for Global Liberty and Prosperity,
    Cato Institute 32
Sophie Richardson, Ph.D., China director, Human Rights Watch 40

LETTERS, STATEMENTS, ETC., SUBMITTED FOR THE HEARING

Perry Link, Ph.D.: Prepared statement 9
Thomas Cushman, Ph.D.: Prepared statement 18
Xia Yeliang, Ph.D.: Prepared statement 35

APPENDIX

Hearing notice...56
Hearing minutes...57
The Honorable Christopher H. Smith, a Representative in Congress from
    the State of New Jersey, and chairman, Subcommittee on Africa, Global
    Health, Global Human Rights, and International Organizations: Letter
    from members of the faculty of New York University 58

IS ACADEMIC FREEDOM THREATENED BY CHINA'S INFLUENCE ON U.S. UNIVERSITIES?

THURSDAY, DECEMBER 4, 2014

House of Representatives,
Subcommittee on Africa, Global Health,
Global Human Rights, and International Organizations,
Committee on Foreign Affairs,
Washington, DC.

The subcommittee met, pursuant to notice, at 1:05 p.m., in room 2172, Rayburn House Office Building, Hon. Christopher H. Smith (chairman of the subcommittee) presiding.

Mr. SMITH. The subcommittee will come to order and good afternoon to everybody.

I welcome you here today. This hearing is the first in a series of hearings probing the question whether China's soft power educational initiatives are undermining academic freedom at U.S. schools and universities.

We see it manifested primarily in two ways. The first is in the building of satellite campuses in China or American universities where Chinese rules of engagement are said to hold sway, in other words, places where no criticism of the Chinese Government or promotions of democracy and freedom are allowed.

Second, we see it in the myriad outposts of Chinese soft power that have opened on campuses throughout the United States and the world, the so-called Confucius Institutes whose curricula integrates Chinese Government policy on contentious issues such as Tibet and Taiwan and whose hiring practices explicitly exclude Falun Gong practitioners. It should be noted that we are seeing emerging faculty opposition to these institutes as well as to the all too cozy and lucrative arrangements which American universities have with institutions affiliated with the Chinese Government.

This prompts us to ask the question: Is American education for sale? And, if so, are U.S. colleges and universities undermining the principle of academic freedom and, in the process, their own credibility in exchange for China's education dollars?

You know, a number of years ago, the author James Mann wrote a book called "The China Fantasy" where he recounts how, in the 1990s, some American business leaders and government officials put forward the fantasy that free trade with China would be the catalyst for political liberalism.

I have been to China many times. I was in China almost immediately after the Tiananmen Square massacre. At one of the meetings in the early 1990s with American businessmen and, despite the ongoing jailing and executions of dissidents, these businessmen in China told me that if we just trade a little more, the dictatorship will somehow matriculate into a democracy. As we all know now, China has failed to democratize, despite increases in the standard of living by many, but certainly not all of its citizens.

Political repression is an all too common occurrence. I have chaired now to date almost 50 Congressional hearings on Chinese human rights abuses. It is not getting better. It is getting demonstrably worse, especially under Xi Jinping. Yet U.S. policy toward China continues to overlook abuses of fundamental human rights for the sake of business opportunities and economic interests.

But what about U.S. universities who often tout their adherence to higher ideals and equate their nonprofit status as a badge of good citizenship, which puts them above reproach. Perhaps they, too, are engaged in their own version of ''The China Fantasy,'' willing to accept limitations in the very principles and freedoms that are the foundation of the U.S. system of higher education, justifying quiet compromises that they would never entertain at home by telling themselves that they are helping to bring about change in China.

As Dr. Perry Link brilliantly argues, these compromises often take the form of self-censorship about what universities and faculty teach, who they invite to speak, what fellows they accept in residence. So long as the dragon is not provoked, they think they will be allowed to continue doing their work, slowly changing China from the inside. But are these American universities changing China or is China changing these American universities?

What is the reason that New York University, for example, terminated the fellowship of a world-class human rights advocate and hero, Chen Guangcheng? NYU was one of those prestigious universities for which China built a campus, a satellite of the University of Shanghai. Though the Chinese Government laid out the funds— and it was a huge amount of money—the transaction involved a moral cost. As certain members of the NYU faculty wrote in a letter to the university board of trustees, the circumstances surrounding the launch of an NYU satellite campus in Shanghai and the ending of Mr. Chen's residence created what they called ''a public perception, accurate or otherwise, that NYU made commitments in order to operate in China.''

I would like, without any objection, to include in the record the letter from the NYU faculty. And without objection, it is so ordered.

I want to note very clearly that we have repeatedly invited NYU's president and key faculty to testify before this subcommittee. And so far, without any success, on five separate occasions, we gave NYU 15 different dates to appear here, to answer serious questions about their relationship with China and, so far, they have begged off on each and every one of them.

This is the first of a series of hearings. I can tell you, we will re-invite NYU and other institutions of higher learning to give an account, to tell us exactly what are those terms and conditions and whether or not they are being muzzled and stifled when it comes to human rights and democracy and other basic freedoms. And I do hope they will come.

3

On a personal note, I spent considerable time with Chen Guangcheng when he first came to the United States, having worked on his case since 2004, which included four congressional hearings exclusively dedicated to his freedom. At two of those hearings, he phoned in from the hospital where he was after he was kicked out of the U.S. Embassy. And at the last one, he said, I want to come to the United States. The next day, the Chinese Government granted him that request.

However, it is my impression that the NYU officials and others sought to isolate him from supporters viewed as too conservative or those they considered Chinese dissidents. We may never know if NYU experienced what Chen himself termed as persistent—and these are his words—"persistent and direct pressure from China to oust him" or if it was simply an act of prudent self-censorship to keep in Beijing's good graces. I don't know the answer. But it is my conviction that self-censorship and the chilling effect that this has had is even more pernicious a threat to fundamental freedoms and to the principle of academic freedom.

One of our witnesses, again, Dr. Perry Link, has made this case repeatedly over the years drawing on his own personal experiences. And I thank him and all of our very distinguished witnesses for being here today.

I would note for the record we are not here to relitigate the sad divorce of Chen Guangcheng and NYU. It is a disheartening part of a larger issue, however, whether American universities will compromise academic freedom again to get a piece of the lucrative Chinese education market.

Today's hearing, then, will mark the beginning of a long hard look of costs and benefits of the growing number of Chinese educational partnerships started by U.S. universities and colleges, including exchange programs and satellite campuses in China and Confucius institutes in the United States and around the world.

While foreign educational partnerships are important endeavors—I was an exchange student, it was a great experience, no one is questioning that—this is a whole different focus. I think we can all agree that U.S. colleges and universities should not be outsourcing academic control, faculty and student oversight, or curriculum to a foreign government, in this case, a dictatorship. Unfortunately, there is now some evidence emerging giving rise to this hearing.

The American Association of University Professors or AAUP, along with its sister organization in Canada, published a report in July blasting the Confucius Institute model as a partnership that "sacrificed the integrity of the [host university] and its academic staff" by requiring "unacceptable concessions" that allow "the Confucius Institutes to advance a state agenda in the recruitment and control of academic staff, in the choice of curriculum, and in the restriction of debate." That is fully their quote.

The AAUP concluded by saying that—and I quote it again—"Confucius Institutes function as an arm of the Chinese state and are allowed to ignore academic freedom" and recommended shutting down U.S. Confucius Institutes unless they could meet certain standards of academic freedom and transparency.

The Confucius Institutes are China's soft power push, an attempt to increase the number of young people studying and ideally, from their point of view, coming to admire, and ours, Chinese culture and language. This is not harmful in itself for the Chinese culture and language, as distinct from its political culture, is indeed admirable.

But while some U.S. university administrators say the influence of Confucius Institutes is benign, University of Chicago's professor Marshall Sahlins has called the Confucius Institutes "academic malware," inimical to the U.S. model of academic freedom.

What we should do is welcome U.S.-China educational partnerships that promote cultural understanding and critical language skills and protect academic freedom, that allow the teaching of sensitive topics and not subject to any of same rules that govern Chinese academic institutions where professors are fired or jailed for exercising the universal right to free speech.

Indeed, there is a U.S. national security interest in having U.S. students learn Chinese, but such language skills should be taught on our terms, without the baggage brought by the Confucius Institute ties. And if those freedoms are violated or compromised, we need to find some recourse, whether through withholding Department of Education funds or State Department exchange program funds from schools that willingly compromise the principles of academic freedom and human rights to gain, again, a small share of the Chinese educational market.

That is why I am announcing today that I will be asking the General Accountability Office (GAO) to study and review the agreements of both satellite campuses in China and of Confucius Institutes in the United States. I would also like to know if those agreements are public, whether they compromise academic or other freedoms of faculty, students, and workers, and whether Chinese teachers are allowed the freedom to worship as they please and to teach about Tiananmen Square, including the massacre, Tibet, or Taiwan.

I will also ask the GAO to study whether U.S. satellite campuses in China operate differently from Chinese universities and whether there is a two-tier system in place where Chinese students and faculty have more restrictions placed on their activities and research than U.S. students and faculties.

I will also ask whether the Communist Party committees operate on campus, whether fundamental freedoms are protected for both Chinese and U.S. students and faculty, again, religious freedom, Internet freedom, freedom of speech, association, and whether universities are required to enforce China's draconian population control policies, particularly on the young women who may be attending those facilities and those institutions.

These are important questions, and there are more. We need to look at whether these issues can be handled by the universities, their faculties and trustees themselves, or if there is something the U.S. Congress and the President must do to ensure that academic freedom is protected. U.S. universities and colleges should reflect and protect the highest principles of freedom and transparency. They should be islands—islands of freedom where foreign students and faculty can enjoy the fundamental freedoms denied them in their own country.

And, again, I want thank our witnesses. And before I introduce to them, yield to my good friend and colleague Mark Meadows for any opening comment.

Mr. MEADOWS. Well, I just thank the chairman for your leadership on this particular issue.

Thank each one of you as witnesses. Certainly, we want to hear from you. There are others that are monitoring this, but I would close with this, human rights—the basic human rights that all of us should enjoy are areas that have really been a hallmark within a lot of our universities in terms of being the beacon of making sure that those voices are heard. And yet here we see, tragically, the reverse potentially being done.

And so as—you heard the passion in the chairman's voice. I can tell you that, whether it is before a camera or whether it is in the privacy of his office where there are just two of us, that passion is consistent and is unyielding.

And so with that, I would yield back, Mr. Chairman.

Mr. SMITH. Thank you very much here, Mr. Meadows.

I would like to now introduce our very distinguished panel, all who have impeccable records but, also, have been true game changers when it comes to human rights.

And I would like to begin first with Dr. Perry Link, who is professor emeritus of east Asian studies at Princeton and Chancellorial chair for teaching across disciplines at the University of California at Riverside. He has published widely on modern Chinese language, literature, and popular thought and is a member of the Princeton China Initiative, Human Rights Watch/Asia, and other groups that support fundamental human rights. He has authored numerous books, and he co-edited with Andrew Nathan ''The Tiananmen Papers, The Chinese Leadership's Decision to Use Force Against Their Own People.'' Since 1996, he has been blacklisted and denied visas by the Chinese Communist Government.

We will then hear from Dr. Thomas Cushman, who is professor in the social studies and professor of sociology the Wellesley College. His academic work has focused on the comparative study of Communist societies with a special emphasis on Communist Party control of civil society and dissidence. He has taught and written extensively on the use of propaganda by authoritarian governments to shape public opinion in liberal democratic societies. He has written and edited numerous books, is a founder and former editor-in-chief of the Journal of Human Rights, and is a prominent activist in the global freedom movement in supporting dissidents in contemporary authoritarian societies.

We will then hear from Dr. Xia Yeliang, who is a visiting professor at the Cato Institute's Center for Global Liberty and Prosperity. Dr. Xia's work focuses on the institutional and policy reforms China needs to become modern, a free society. Prior to joining Cato, Dr. Xia was a professor in the department of economics at Peking University where he taught since 2000. He was dismissed by Peking University in October 2013 because of his outspoken criticism of China's Communist Party and his advocacy of

6

democracy and basic human rights. Dr. Xia was among the original signers of Charter 08, a 2008 manifesto calling for basic freedoms, constitutional democracy, and respect for human rights, and was a founder of the Cathay Institute of Public Affairs, a market-liberal think-tank in China.

We will then hear from Dr. Sophie Richardson, who is no stranger to this subcommittee, who is China director at Human Rights Watch. Dr. Richardson is the author of numerous articles on domestic Chinese political reform and democratization and human rights in many Asian countries. She has testified before the European Parliament, the U.S. Congress, this subcommittee many times, as well as others, and has provided commentary to many prominent news outlets. Dr. Richardson is the author of ''China, Cambodia, and the Five Principles of Peaceful Coexistence,'' an in-depth examination of China's foreign policy since 1954's Geneva Conference, including rare interviews with policymakers.

Just an extraordinary panel. And, Dr. Perry Link, I would like to yield to you such time as you may consume.

STATEMENT OF PERRY LINK, PH.D., CHANCELLORIAL CHAIR FOR INNOVATIVE TEACHING, UNIVERSITY OF CALIFORNIA, RIVERSIDE

Mr. LINK. Thank you, Mr. Chairman, and Congressman Meadows, for inviting me to this important hearing.

In academic exchange with China, our country has two very different kinds of interlocutors on the other side. These are, number one, the officials of the Communist Party of China and, two, Chinese scholars themselves. And it is crucial to distinguish these two different players. Most of the mistakes of U.S. academic administrators come from a failure to distinguish them. The two groups have different goals. The main goal of the Chinese scholars, like scholars everywhere, is to advance knowledge.

The main goals of the Communist Party are three: First, to gain technological knowledge that will be useful in increasing the power of the Chinese state. Second, to spread abroad a rosy version of Chinese history that is incomplete and, in important respects, false. And, third, to intimidate and to punish scholars, both Chinese and Western, who do not cooperate.

It is crucially important to recognize the nonscholarly goals of the Communist Party of China and, hence, to be careful in scholarly exchange. But it would also be a serious mistake to turn away from China's genuine scholars who have come under increasingly severe pressure in recent months. The Chinese Government has issued orders nationwide that scholars must support the Communist Party and reject so-called universal values. Chinese scholars who disobey are subject to harassment, firings, and even imprisonment.

The political persecution of scholars in China today is worse than it has been since the 1970s under Mao Zedong. This persecution is part of a larger pattern of aggressive behavior by the Chinese state on many fronts. One of the many costs of the troubles in the Middle East is that it is distracting attention from the serious trouble that is brewing today in China.

Inside China, for decades, the main tool by which the Communist Party has controlled expression has been to use fear to induce self-censorship. ''Don't say what we do not want to hear or you will bear the consequences.'' Now, with China's new wealth and rise on the world stage, the Chinese Communist Party has sought to apply these same tools in other countries, including ours. The effects are visible in business and diplomacy, but here I will restrict my comments to academics.

Western scholars, like myself, are made to understand that if they cross red lines in their public expression, if they mention topics such as Tibetan or Uyghur autonomy, Taiwan independence, the Falun Gong, the Tiananmen massacre, Chinese imprisoning the Nobel Peace laureate Liu Xiaobo, the spectacular wealth of the superelite families of Xi Jinping, Li Peng, Wen Jiabao and others, then, they will have trouble. Their access to field work, archives, and interviews might be blocked and they can be blacklisted from entering the country entirely.

At any given time, there are only a dozen or two American scholars on visa blacklists but the effect of the blacklists extends much, much farther because virtually every scholar knows about the blacklists and has an incentive to stay clear of the red lines. This pressure affects the way American scholars use language, and here there are major costs to the American public. Because, for example, Beijing forbids mention of Taiwan independence, scholars speak of ''the Taiwan question'' or ''cross-strait issues.'' Similarly, the Tiananmen massacre becomes only ''an incident.'' Graduate students are counseled not to write dissertations about Chinese democracy for fear that blacklisting might ruin their young careers. Seasoned scholars are afraid to go on the PBS News Hour to comment on politically sensitive topics.

In addition to fear as a way to induce self-censorship, in recent times, the Chinese Government has used positive inducements to similar effect. It has funded an archipelago of Confucius Institutes to teach Chinese language and culture in colleges and high schools around the world, including more than 70 in our country. American recipients of these funds know, without having to be told, that they must not invite the Dalai Lama, hold seminars on Liu Xiaobo, or cross other Communist Party red lines. A wordless self-censorship reigns. And students see only a blanched cameo of what China is today.

Now, I am trying to stay under 5 minutes, so I am going to name my three policy recommendations in brief. But you can read more about them in my written statements.

Mr. SMITH. Again, if——

Mr. LINK. Pardon?

Mr. SMITH [continuing]. Any of you exceed the 5, we are more than happy to receive it orally as well. So don't limit yourself too much, okay.

Mr. LINK. My first policy recommendation is that the U.S. Government should fund Chinese language programs in the U.S. Our chairman himself mentioned this a moment ago. Why should we—and by ''we'' I mean school administrators across the country—hand our young people over to an authoritarian government because they supply the funds? We have enough funds for that. Certainly, this should be a vital national interest.

My second recommendation is that American university administrators, in their programs with China, should adopt a policy of consciously staking out the broadest of fields. What I mean by that is that, when a satellite campus is set up in Shanghai or somewhere or a Confucius Institute here, the policy ought to be to make it clear in a low-key but dignified way that we will talk about Liu Xiaobo, we will talk about the Tiananmen massacre, we will have seminars with the Dalai Lama, if we can get him to come, not for the purpose of sticking our fingers in the dragon's eye, but in order to stake out the borderline. Because if you don't stake out the borderline, natural self-censorship will kick in and the field with shrink, shrink, shrink, shrink, shrink, until you are saying nothing except that blanched cameo.

The third recommendation I have is that the U.S. Government should withhold visas for Confucius Institute instructors at high profile U.S. institutions until the practice of withholding visas for American scholars on political grounds is ended.

And I will stop there. Thank you, Mr. Chairman.

Mr. SMITH. Thank you so very much, Dr. Link.

[The prepared statement of Mr. Link follows:]

Testimony of Perry Link

**Chancellorial Chair at the University of California,
Riverside**

at the hearing on

"Is Academic Freedom Threatened by China's

Influence on American Universities?"

U.S. House Committee on Foreign Affairs

December 4, 2014

I. **The Costs and Benefits of Academic Exchange with China**

Since the "opening" of China following the death of Mao Zedong in the late 1970s, academics in China have sought to connect with their colleagues in the outside world. This is an entirely natural and healthful aspiration, one that scholars around the world have rightly supported. The resultant exchanges have benefited Chinese scholars and scholars everywhere.

This kind of exchange, scholar-to-scholar, in pursuit of objective knowledge, needs to be sharply distinguished from the programs of the Communist Party of China (CPC), which has continuously exercised one-party dictatorship over all programs of the Chinese government and whose goals are to advance its own power interests.

Two kinds of people—Chinese scholars and representatives of the CPC—have been involved in what both call "academic exchange" with the U.S. and other countries. It is crucial to understand the distinction between these two players and to appreciate their different motives. For U.S. academic administrators who are unfamiliar with China, observation of the distinction is made more difficult by the fact that some interlocutors on the Chinese side are a mixture of genuine scholar and CPC spokesperson, while many others, although genuine scholars underneath, are obliged to speak for the CPC out of fear of the consequences if they do not.

A common, almost universal, mistake among U.S. academic administrators is to accept the CPC as the authentic voice of "the other side." This acceptance puts the power interests of a one-party dictatorship in a place where universal pursuit of truth should be. The CPC's power interests include these:

--to obtain advanced technical know-how in service of strengthening the Chinese state;

--to spread abroad a version of Chinese history that is incomplete and on important points false;

--to intimidate and to punish scholars, both Chinese and Western, who do not cooperate in these goals.

The international community makes a grievous mistake when it fails to recognize the non-scholarly goals of the CPC; but it also makes a serious mistake if, in deterring the CPC's parries, it forgets about genuine Chinese scholars.

Inexperienced academic administrators in the U.S. often draw up campus-to-campus "protocols" or "memoranda of understanding" with CPC officials. These are useful to CPC officials as credentials in their quest for prestige and funding within the Chinese context, but they do little if anything for genuine scholarly exchange. Genuine exchange happens when scholars themselves are moved to cooperate and take the initiatives themselves. This kind of scholarly collaboration, "from below," should be encouraged. But U.S. administrators should be aware that the CPC has always feared and opposed scholarly cooperation of this kind, because of its independent origins.

Scholars in China have come under sharply increased pressure in recent months. Unsubtle guidelines that university professors must be "patriotic" (i.e., support the CPC) and must oppose ideas like "universal values" have been spread all across the country. The orders have been broadly obeyed, in part because of the punishments that disobedience brings. The few scholars who dare not to obey have been monitored, threatened, harassed, fired, beaten, indicted, or imprisoned—the degree of their punishment calibrated to the degree to which they persist in their dissent. Individual American scholars often speak out for their Chinese colleagues under pressure, but American academic administrators seldom do, and formal cooperation with the CPC—the oppressing party—marches forward. This is not because U.S. academic administrators are illiberal in their values; it is because they do not understand the realities of the Chinese side and are insufficiently diligent in discovering them.

II. Harmful Influences of the Chinese Government on American Academic Freedom

For decades, the primary strategy of the CPC in censoring its own people has been to induce self-censorship. This has normally been achieved through fear: "say what you know we want to hear, or suffer the consequences"—which could be humiliation, job loss, imprisonment, and even death. In recent times, with the rise of the economy, the CPC has turned to positive inducements as well: "stay in bounds, join us, and you can have money, status, and a share of power." But regardless of whether carrots or sticks are used, the key has been to engineer people into positions where they censor themselves willingly.

Now the CPC, stronger and wealthier than before, is looking to project these battle-tested methods onto the world stage. It uses both punishments and inducements to prevent unwanted expression. The techniques operate in many spheres, including business and diplomacy, but here I will comment only on the academic sphere. NOTE: These techniques are not just matters of "threat"; they have been in operation for years.

Punishments. American scholars who study China need access to the country. The CPC, knowing this, uses visa denials, blockage of access to archives or fieldwork, and other means, subtle and unsubtle, to make it clear that people who write or say things "unfriendly" to the CPC will have troubles. Blacklisted American scholars are sometimes summoned to Chinese consulates where they are told directly that they need to be less critical of the Chinese government if they want to travel to China. (Genuine Chinese scholars do not display this attitude; with very rare exceptions, they are open and welcoming of American scholars.)

It is crucial to understand that actual blockage of U.S. scholars is a much smaller problem than the pervasive *fear* of blockage. The number of American China scholars on visa blacklists is only a dozen or two at any given time, but the number who watch their words in order to *avoid* possible blacklisting is in the thousands. Indeed, such avoidance is the norm. I have been on a visa blacklist since the mid-1990s, and I hear, on average, two or three inquiries per month from younger scholars who want to know what they should avoid saying in order not to end up where I am.

Visa denials are the CPC's strongest tools of punishment, but the others—blocking access to archives, fieldwork, or interviews—operate similarly.

Inducements. In recent years the CPC has offered funds to university and high-school campuses around the world, including in the U.S., to establish "Confucius Institutes" and other CPC-funded joint projects in teaching and research. American school administrators, always looking for more funding, have been largely receptive. Many have allowed CPC authorities in Beijing to choose teachers and set curricula on their campuses.

Teaching in the Confucius Institutes is primarily of Chinese language and cultural topics that have little relation to one-party rule by the CPC. American academic administrators who accept CPC funds point to this fact when they say they are importing no political biases. The CPC uses this anodyne approach to gain acceptance on campuses; its others goals—of spreading a false image of itself and of Chinese history—are achieved largely by two other means:

1. The teachers at Confucius Institutes are selected and trained to present pro-CPC versions of Chinese history and society in all contexts, formal and informal, while they are abroad. The degree to which they do this willingly is irrelevant to the fact that they will be held responsible if they do not do it correctly.

2. American administrators who accept CPC funds understand, without needing to be directly told, that topics the CPC does not welcome—such as Tibetan or Uighur autonomy, Taiwan independence, Occupy Central in Hong Kong, the Falun Gong, underground Christian churches, the Tiananmen massacre, China's imprisoned Nobel Peace Laureate, the spectacular wealth of the families of Xi Jinping, Li Peng, Wen Jiabao, and others in the super-elite, and more (the list is constantly changing and growing)—will not be sponsored by Confucius Institutes. Money-induced self-censorship prevents even the suggestion of such topics. American students are presented a roseate cameo of China and are told that it is the whole. Omission of the forbidden topics not only reduces the size of the picture; it misrepresents the character of the part that remains.

Some academic administrators in the U.S. have acknowledged the cameo problem but say that it does not matter because healthy university campuses have many other sources of information about China that can serve as needed correctives. This is true for large campuses (less so for small ones, or high schools), but it seems an odd argument to make. Should you do something harmful because you are confident that something beneficial can outweigh it? Do you cut off a finger because, after all, you have nine others?

III. Costs to the U.S. and the International Community

When American scholars cannot go to China to do their interviewing or field study, or to visit archives, there are real costs to their work. But, as noted above, these costs are small compared to the very much larger problem of the widespread self-censorship that results from fear of being blacklisted. Here are some representative examples (all factual, although I omit names):

--A brilliant Ph.D. student wants to write a dissertation about Chinese democracy, but his well-meaning advisers counsel against it; it could get him blacklisted and ruin his budding career; he settles for a tamer topic.

--A seasoned historian, who has written on the ideologies of Chinese rebel movements, is invited to the PBS Newshour to discuss the Falun Gong. She declines; it could complicate her research access in China; the U.S. public hears from a second-best authority on the Newshour.

--An idealistic undergraduate gets a summer internship with Human Rights Watch; later she hears that such a thing on her record might bar her from China; she declines the internship. (In this case, and many others, self-censorship goes far beyond what is needed.)

Yet even cases like these, of which there are many, do not make clear the most widespread costs of academic self-censorship about China. The widest costs are in language use. China scholars know that if you are writing about politics in Taiwan, you do not speak of Taiwan independence but of the "the Taiwan question"; the Tiananmen massacre was not a massacre but an "incident" or an "event"; China's super-rich may be corrupt but, please, let's avoid naming names. And most important, while observing CPC red lines, speak and write about as if the red lines were not there.

China scholars sometimes point out that this kind of circumspection in their expression is only a code of convenience. Everyone is clear about what the term "Taiwan question" really refers to, so why stick a finger in the dragon's eye by bringing up the word "independence"? This point is fair enough, as long as it is inside the club of China scholars. The problem—and it is a large one—is that the code words are not shed when scholars step outside their club to address students in a classroom or the public over the airwaves or in cyberspace. Will the public be able to guess what the Taiwan "question" really is? Will it know that an "incident" in 1989 was actually a massacre? Many people in the Chinese public under twenty years of age already do not know about that massacre; it is a goal of the CPC that the American and international public not know about it, either.

Thirty years ago Americans could look at the CPC's repression of speech, assembly, and publication inside China and, from a distance, feel empathy for the Chinese people. Today the luxury of distance is gone. The CPC has brought its engineering techniques to U.S. shores and is setting up shop.

IV. Policy recommendations

1. *The U.S. government should fund Chinese-language programs in the U.S.* Why should American campuses that need such programs have to turn for support to the CPC and its campaign to make the world safe for autocrats—even at the risk of misleading the American young? Why don't we meet the CPC challenge where it is being made? A single B-2 Spirit

Bomber reportedly costs about $2.4 billion. That amount would provide far more than adequate funding to every American campus that needs an honest Chinese language program—and very arguably do more to blunt the CPC's advance than the airplane could.

2. *American university administrators, in their programs with China, should adopt a policy of "consciously staking out the broadest of fields."* By this I mean that they should say, and should show in their actions, right at the outset, in a dignified but clear way, that specific topics like the Dalai Lama, the imprisoned Nobel laureate, the Tiananmen massacre, and others, will be in bounds in the exchange. They should make periodic efforts to re-insert these topics (or to support Chinese and American scholars who wish to insert them). The reason for this policy is not to pick fights with CPC representatives, and it is fine to make clear that belligerence is not the motive. The absolutely crucial reason for the policy is that, if it is not there, then the CPC's mechanisms of induced self-censorship will take over, the scope of "mentionable" topics will contract, the contracted field will come to seem "normal," and academic freedom will die.

3. *The U.S. government should withhold visas for Confucius Institute instructors at high-profile U.S. institutions until the practice of withholding visas for American scholars on political grounds is ended.*

V. The Larger Context

The policies of the CPC since the ascension of Xi Jinping two years ago have become intensely more ominous. The crackdown on press freedom and academic freedom inside China is worse than anything we have seen since Mao Zedong, and it is clear that Xi is looking to project the CPC's power globally.

Xi, though, is no Mao, in either intellect or force of personality, and it is an open question whether his juggernaut will crash or soar. Whichever happens, the consequences for the American people, and people everywhere, could be severe. One of the many costs of the troubles in the Middle East is that it has distracted attention from the trouble that is quite clearly brewing in China.

15

Mr. SMITH. We now go to Dr. Cushman.

STATEMENT OF THOMAS CUSHMAN, PH.D., DEFFENBAUGH DE HOYOS CARLSON CHAIR IN THE SOCIAL SCIENCES, WELLESLEY COLLEGE

Mr. CUSHMAN. I would like to thank the committee, and Mr. Chairman and Mr. Meadows, for inviting me to provide testimony today.

My comments are a very brief overview of a more detailed written testimony submitted for the record.

We have already talked about Confucius Institutes, satellite campuses. My concern has been with the more small-scale partnerships being forged out between the United States and Chinese institutions involving exchanges of students and faculty in special events around common themes. We have much less data on the nature and structure of these relationships, but I feel like they are one of the more important emerging structural relationships between U.S. and Chinese institutions.

Just last week, Chinese President Xi Jinping noted that the Chinese foreign policy should be designed to "increase China's soft power, give a good Chinese narrative, and better communicate China's message to the world." It should be stressed at the outset that partnerships between U.S. and Chinese academic institutions will be a major means for promoting this Chinese foreign policy objective.

I would also like to raise the question, perhaps rhetorically, of what does it mean for U.S. institutions to enter into a literal partnership with the Chinese Communist Party. On the U.S. side, institutions of higher education are a main mechanism of the 100,000 strong initiative put forth by the Obama administration in 2009.

China is a rich source of revenue from the estimated 274,000 Chinese students studying in the U.S. The vast majority of whom paid full tuition and costs. Students from the PRC contribute an estimated $27 billion per annum to the American economy. Most of the attention to date in a scholarly way has been focused on Confucius Institutes. As I said, my concern is with the more general partnerships that we really have very little data on, but that I am starting to collect.

Based on my own experiences and research, I would like to raise some concerns about these new partnerships in answer to the central question of the hearing, is academic freedom threatened by Chinese influence in universities? And many of my observations mirror those of Professor Link and, I am sure, others on the panel and elsewhere.

Number one, formal exchanges and partnerships provide platforms for official positions of the CCP to be aired on U.S. campuses and at formal events in China. At many academic events, whether in China or the U.S., one can expect the presence of representatives of the CCP, who monitor events, engage in surveillance of Chinese participants and, when possible, use such events for official propaganda purposes.

Two—and this has been covered already—but institutions and programs in the U.S. may decide not to cover certain topics during official events because of concern for offending or being rude to their Chinese counterparts or because of direct pressure from the Chinese side.

Three, scholars of China may self-censor and avoid public criticism of aspects of China for fear of losing access to China. And this has been already gone over, so I won't mention it again.

Fourth, the partnerships are asymmetrical. U.S. scholars are subject to close scrutiny for their work and face potential bans from China, whereas Chinese scholars are free from such constraints and can, theoretically, discuss the problems of American society with impunity. And given that the cultural climate in American universities, you might actually add that Chinese scholars who come and criticize the United States would be welcomed, as opposed to U.S. scholars going to criticize aspects of Chinese society.

Fifth, for many U.S. faculty members of Chinese origin, exchanges between U.S. institutions—between their institutions in the U.S. and their home country represent intercultural opportunities that could not be dreamed of just a short time ago. Chinese faculty members in the United States are building important bridges between the U.S. and China that are necessary, but some might be less hesitant to criticize China in order to protect these new opportunities, to protect their own access to China, and especially, from what I have been able to determine, to protect family members who remain there.

Sixth, professors who are increasing subject to student evaluations for promotion, tenure, and salary increases, especially at the junior levels, may avoid discussing sensitive topics about China in their classes out of fear of negative evaluations by Chinese students who are understandably defensive and patriotic about China.

Seven, professors who are publically critical of particular practices in China, especially those of the CCP, run the risk of being labeled as anti-China or anti-Chinese. This deliberate propaganda tactic of equating criticism of the policies of the CCP with criticisms of persons of Chinese or more general Asian descent is especially effective in the current climate of identity politics that predominates on American campuses.

The fundamental duty of all U.S. universities is the protection of academic freedom as the inalienable moral foundation of the modern university. In order to protect infringements on academic freedom that might ensue from partnerships with Chinese institutions, professors must take a leading role in, first, fostering debates on controversial issues that are avoided on campuses, especially in resistance to people who might try to stop them.

Two, exposing deliberate CCP propaganda efforts associated with events carried out in the U.S. under the aegis of partnerships. This task can be enhanced by drawing on the considerable experience and expertise of Chinese dissidents and human rights activists and inviting them to campuses at every available opportunity, again, with the coda that there might be resistance to such things.

Third, providing Chinese students with the tools for critical thinking that are the core of the liberal arts, while at the same time understanding and respecting their views and experiences as students who are educated in an environment where independent and critical thinking are highly circumscribed.

17

Fourth, developing courses that deliberately examine controversial topics that are avoided in China and which other faculty in the U.S. environment might not teach in order to avoid giving offense, again, with the coda that there might be resistance to such things.

In my full written report to the subcommittee, I have made several policy recommendations for your consideration, one of which I will mention—that I think that one thing we don't know and that, I think, that political authorities might be concerned in finding out—is among institutions who receive Federal funding for their programs in no matter what form, there should be some kind of audit or kind of inventory of exactly how many American universities have what kind of partnerships with China, what is discussed at these partnerships. This is an extremely important thing. We just simply don't know how many there are.

And I also suggest that colleges themselves and universities who receive Federal funds who somehow get money from the Government for any of their programs should also ensure that there are yearly audits of things that go on in their own campuses which demonstrate to the rest of the world and academia and even people like this committee that there is legitimate academic freedom and efforts to protect academic freedom on American campuses.

Thank you very much.

Mr. SMITH. Mr. Cushman, thank you very much for your excellent testimony and your leadership and you and the other professors who bravely stood up for Dr. Xia, who is our next witness.

[The prepared statement of Mr. Cushman follows:]

December 2, 2014

Thomas Cushman
House Committee on Foreign Affairs, Subcommittee on Africa, Global
Human Rights, and International Organizations
December 4, 2014: "Is Academic Freedom Threatened by China's
Influence on U.S. Universities?"

I am honored by the invitation of the U.S. House of Representatives House Committee on Foreign Affairs, Subcommittee on Africa, Global Human Rights, and International Organizations. I am here today, first and foremost, as a citizen who wishes to comment on exchanges and partnerships between U.S. and Chinese institutions of higher education and their possible implications for academic freedom in U.S. institutions.

My testimony is not motivated by any animus toward China, the Chinese people, or the outstanding students from the PRC whom it has been my distinct honor and pleasure to teach. My career as a scholar and human rights activist over the course of 30 years has focused on authoritarian regimes and their repression of fundamental human rights and liberties. My activities have focused on studying dissidents in authoritarian societies who are at risk and assisting them in their efforts to promote freedom. I have been an ardent supporter of Professor Xia Yeliang, the dissident economist, who was terminated from his post at Peking University in fall of 2013 for political reasons.

I was one of seven Wellesley professors who wrote an Open Letter to Peking University to protest the firing of Professor Xia.[1] This letter was signed by over 140 Wellesley faculty members, and served as a basis for a very contentious debate on the Wellesley-PKU partnership, which was formally instituted in June of 2013. I sought, unsuccessfully, to secure for him a two-year visiting scholar-in-residence position in the Department of Sociology and the Freedom Project at Wellesley College. He is currently a two-year

---

[1]http://www.boston.com/yourcampus/news/OpenLetterPekingUniversityXiaY
eliang.pdf

Visiting Associate of The Freedom Project and in October, 2014 was awarded the annual Freedom Project Award for Civil Courage.

In recent years, many US institutions of higher education have entered into formal relations with Chinese universities. These have ranged from large-scale institutional efforts involving "bricks and mortar" satellite campuses in China (e.g. Duke Kunshan University, New York University Shanghai) to relatively small-scale partnerships that involve exchanges of students and faculty and special events around common themes. From a scholarly perspective, such relations are vitally important in an increasingly globalized and interconnected world and should be maintained. No serious scholar could argue that the U.S should not have such relations with China. However, there are several troubling aspects of these relations that may infringe upon academic freedom in American universities, and more generally on the right of freedom of expression guaranteed by the First Amendment of the U.S. Constitution.

The Chinese government's effort to developing extensive formal relations with U.S institutions is part of a more general "soft power" strategy toward the West. The aim is to partner with U.S. educational institutions at all levels to gain legitimacy abroad for China, in general, and to enhance the prestige of Chinese institutions of higher education, in particular. These partnerships work to "normalize" Chinese universities by using the prestige of American universities to build their own prestige in world university rankings. They also work to establish an official presence in American higher education that can work to achieve the propaganda goals of the CCP. This propaganda strategy was openly admitted by Liu Yunshan, Minister of Propaganda, in January 2010, who stressed that "we should actively carry out international propaganda battles against issues such as Tibet, Xinjiang, Taiwan, Human Rights, and Falun Gong." [2] In addition, new cadres of

---

[2] Quoted in Marshall Sahlins, Marshall Sahlins, *Confucius Institutes: Academic Malware* (Chicago: Prickly Paradigm Press, 2014), p. 6. The original speech at Yongning Government Website is inaccessible as of November 28, 2014:
http://yongning.gov.cn/ynkxfg/contents/265/2221_5.html

current and future Chinese elites gain legitimacy from acquiring degrees from U.S. institutions and such degrees are important credentials for personal advancement and mobility in Chinese society. Given the control of Chinese universities by the Communist Party of China, and the intensification of repression of freedom of thought and expression with the ascent of Xi Jinping, partnerships cannot in any way be seen from the official point of view as means for the liberalization of intellectual life in China.

On the U.S. side, exchanges with China are beneficial to U.S. interests for learning more about China, a necessity given its emergence as a world power. There is no better way for young people in the U.S. to learn about their counterparts in China than sustained and vigorous interactions with them. U.S. institutions of higher education are a main mechanism of the 100,000 Strong Initiative put forth by the Obama administration in 2009. [3] China is a rich source of revenue from the estimated 274,000 Chinese students studying in the US, the vast number of whom pay full tuition and costs.[4] Students from the PRC bring huge benefits to the US economy, which are estimated by the Institute of International Education at $27 billion per annum.[5]

It is neither possible nor desirable from a financial or cultural point of view to restrict formal educational programs with China, or the number of Chinese students coming to the U.S. There are distinct benefits to large numbers of Chinese students being exposed to an American society and to American ideas of rights and freedom that could be the source of positive social change in China. However, the expansion of partnerships between U.S. and Chinese institutions are taking place in a period of intensifying political repression of freedom of expression in China. Last year, Chinese president

---

[3] See the Institute for International Education report at: http://www.iie.org/Research-and-Publications/Publications-and-Reports/IIE-Bookstore/US-Students-in-China

[4] http://www.iie.org/Who-We-Are/News-and-Events/Press-Center/Press-Releases/2014/2014-11-17-Open-Doors-Data

[5] http://www.iie.org/Who-We-Are/News-and-Events/Press-Center/Press-Releases/2014/2014-11-17-Open-Doors-Data

Xi Jinping, issued a formal declaration of forbidden topics that are central ideas in the Western tradition of liberal democracy: universal values, freedom of speech, civil society, civil and political rights, the historical errors of the CCP, crony capitalism, and judicial independence. [6] He declared an overt war on independent intellectuals, asserting that "We must strike hard at handful of reactionary intellectuals making use of the Internet to spread rumors, attack, and slander the CCP's rule, the socialist system, and the national regime. " [7] There has been an increase in the persecution, firing and imprisonment of critics of the CCP and its policies, including, most recently, the high profile case of Ilham Tohti, the Uighur professor of economics, who is now serving a life sentence for "separatism". [8]

The general strategy of the CCP allows for some limited freedom of expression in small-scale social environments, but restricts severely such expression when it becomes more diffuse in the public sphere. [9] The Chinese Communist Youth League exerts tight control over student freedom of expression in Chinese universities through strict procedural controls as well as surveillance and intimidation of those who cross the boundaries of tolerable public discussion. [10] American students may experience some degree of openness in small-scale settings, and perhaps perceive that there is a high degree of public freedom of expression. They may be unaware of more repressive limitations on freedom of expression in the public sphere, or worse, believe that public criticism and civil society activism are, in fact,

---

[6] http://www.globalpost.com/dispatch/news/regions/asia-pacific/china/130529/censorship-chinese-communist-party
[7] http://www.straitstimes.com/the-big-story/asia-report/opinion/story/xi-wages-ideological-war-against-liberals-20130925
[8] http://www.hrw.org/news/2014/09/15/timeline-ilham-tohti-s-case
[9] King, Gary, Jennifer Pan, and Margaret E Roberts. 2013. "How Censorship in China Allows Government Criticism but Silences Collective Expression," *American Political Science Review* 107, no. 2 (May): 1-18 http://gking.harvard.edu/publications/how-censorship-china-allows-government-criticism-silences-collective-expression
[10] http://articles.latimes.com/2012/dec/09/world/la-fg-china-students-20121209

"rude", "wrong," or "offensive" and should be avoided. American students are compelled to engage self-censorship in public debates, as the Chinese people themselves must do. To do otherwise could constitute violations of Chinese law that criminalize public expression of controversial views, i.e., "creating public disturbances", "illegal assembly", etc.

There seems little that can be done from the U.S. side, by academics, to counter repression of freedom of expression within China. It is improbable, if not impossible, for American academics in China to push for open and public discussion of forbidden topics. It should be stressed that many professors may feel that this is inappropriate, especially if their research has nothing to do with sensitive political topics. They should be respected in this position. Overall, the essential precondition of the academic presence in the Chinese environment is a tacit agreement to engage in self-censorship.

There is much that academics can do, however, to ensure that there is maximal freedom of expression in American institutions of higher education. The moral imperative for U.S. universities – administrators and faculty alike – is to ensure that freedom of expression is not infringed upon because of the need to maintain formal relations with Chinese counterparts and the tangible material benefits that accrue from such relations.

American scholars are beginning to examine how relations with Chinese institutions have led to clear patterns of overt censorship and self-censorship on American campuses. [11] A focus of recent attention is The Confucius Institutes (CIs), of which there are an estimated 100 in the US, including at such prestigious universities as Stanford, Columbia, and, up until recently, The University of Chicago. The large majority of CIs are at state universities, many of which welcome the funds provided by the Chinese government in light of fiscal crises in the states that have reduced spending on higher education.[12] The American Association of University Professors "Committee

---

[11] See, for instance, Marshall Sahlins, *Confucius Institutes: Academic Malware* (Chicago: Prickly Paradigm Press, 2014).

[12] A list of Confucius Institutes in the U.S., which ought to be continually checked and updated, can be found at:

A on Academic Freedom and Tenure" issued a statement in Confucius Institutes issued a statement in June 2014, calling for increased scrutiny of CIs.[13] The report notes that:

> Confucius Institutes function as an arm of the Chinese state and are allowed to ignore academic freedom. Their academic activities are under the supervision of Hanban, a Chinese state agency which is chaired by a member of the Politburo and the vice-premier of the People's Republic of China. Most agreements establishing Confucius Institutes feature nondisclosure clauses and unacceptable concessions to the political aims and practices of the government of China. Specifically, North American universities permit Confucius Institutes to advance a state agenda in the recruitment and control of academic staff, in the choice of curriculum, and in the restriction of debate.

The report calls for ensuring that American universities exercise unilateral control over CIs, guarantee academic freedom for CI employees, and make all university-Hanban agreements available to "all members of the university community." An important part of the report is the concluding statement, which states that... *"More generally, these conditions should apply to any partnerships or collaborations with foreign governments or foreign government-related agencies* (emphasis added).*"*[15]

The CIs are only the most obvious institutional partnerships between China and the US, and have garnered the most attention. More common, smaller-scale, and less institutionalized partnerships and exchanges have emerged, however, without adequate consideration of the same issues that have been raised regarding CIs. The usual process for establishing a partnership between a U.S. and Chinese institution is to sign a "Memorandum of Understanding" (MOU), in which common goals and plans are specified.

---

http://confucius.gmu.edu/upload/Resources_Alphabetical-list-of-Confucius-Institutes-in-the-USA.pdf

[13] http://www.aaup.org/report/confucius-institutes

[14] http://www.aaup.org/report/confucius-institutes

[15] http://www.aaup.org/report/confucius-institutes

These are essentially loose contracts that appear to have no legal status, and there is no one type of MOU. At the present time, it is difficult to know exactly how many partnerships have been established between U.S. and Chinese institutions. To the best of my knowledge, the process of forming partnerships is unregulated by any political authority and they are usually initiated and carried out by academic administrators in non-transparent negotiations, which are then announced to faculty.

The central questions about partnerships are:

1. How might academic freedom and freedom of expression, more generally, in American universities and colleges be affected by these formal partnerships with the Chinese government and the Communist Party of China?

2. What does it mean for institutions of higher education in a liberal democratic society to be in "partnerships" with an authoritarian, one-party regime?

3. What does it mean that many of these partnerships claim they are committed to academic freedom and liberalization at a particular time in history when the CCP is intensifying its programs of "thought management" in Chinese universities, and increasing repression of independent and dissident voices in civil society?

The formation of partnerships with Chinese universities has far outpaced the development of procedures and mechanisms for the monitoring and protection of academic freedom on American campuses. The fundamental task of all U.S. universities ought to be the protection of academic freedom as the most fundamental, non-negotiable foundations of the modern university. While there are usually mentions of "academic freedom" in MOUs that establish formal partnerships, these appear to be purely rhetorical and symbolic, and specify no procedures for monitoring and ensuring the exercise of academic freedom.

Central Concerns Regarding Partnerships

Based on my own experiences with the Wellesley-PKU partnership, and on sociological observations in the more general American (and in some cases the European environment), I offer the following concerns in answer to the central question: *Is academic freedom threatened by Chinese influence in U.S. universities?* The word "threatened" is perhaps too strong as a general term to describe all the potentially negative effects of Chinese influence, though, in some cases, it might be appropriate. Perhaps a more appropriate concern, taken from the language of the U.S. Constitution, should be on the possible and actual *infringements* of academic freedom.

1. Formal exchanges and partnerships provide platforms for official positions of the CCP to be aired on US campuses and at formal events in China. At many academic events, whether in China or the US, one can expect the presence of representatives of the CCP who monitor events, engage in surveillance of Chinese participants, and, when possible, use such events for official propaganda purposes.

2. Institutions and programs may decide not to cover certain topics because of concern for offending or being "rude" to their Chinese counterparts. This possibility is enhanced by the culture of civility in China in which public criticism of any aspect of Chinese society causes China to "lose face." There are numerous cases in which American professors admit openly to self-censorship and to consciously limiting the discussion of controversial issues such as Tibet (and the Dalai Lama), Taiwan, human rights, dissidents, or ethic and nationalities problems. [16] The most serious consequence of this is that the realities of repression and violations of fundamental human rights in China become hidden beneath a "beautified" version of China, making these repressions and violations all the more effective. In a recent pronouncement, President Xi Jinping noted that Chinese foreign policy should be designed to "increase China's soft power, give a good Chinese narrative and better communicate

---

[16] See, for examples, Sahlins, op.cit.

China's message to the world." [17] *It should be stressed that partnerships between Chinese and U.S. academic institutions will be a major means for promoting this foreign policy objective.*

3. Scholars of China may self-censor and avoid public criticism of aspects of China for fear of losing access to China. That this happens is well known in the community of Western Sinologists, many of whom are banned from entering China for writing critically about aspects of Chinese society. [18] This constant fear of losing access serves as a strong motivation for self-censorship. Very often, this self-censorship is subtle. For instance, when a group of Harvard University professors invited the dissident poet, Liao Yiwu, to read his emotional and controversial poem about Tiananmen Square, "Massacre," gave him private accolades for doing it, but declined to put a video of it on their website.[19]

4. This process is also asymmetrical: US scholars are subject to close scrutiny for their work and banned from China, whereas Chinese scholars are free from such constraints and can, theoretically, discuss the problems of American society with impunity. This is a general problem of open societies: they must allow the expression of ideas and values that are critical of them, whereas closed societies operate under no such constraints. Given the dominance of perspectives that are critical of America in U.S. universities, they are likely to find support for doing so. Chinese propagandists are very skillful in raising the specter of Western imperialism, U.S. hegemony, the ill- treatment of Chinese and other Asian populations in American history, and other topics that are of central

---

[17] http://www.nytimes.com/2014/12/01/world/asia/leader-asserts-chinas-growing-role-on-global-stage.html?_r=0

[18] See, for example, http://www.bloomberg.com/news/2011-08-11/china-banning-u-s-professors-elicits-silence-from-colleges.html and http://www.nytimes.com/2014/07/08/world/asia/us-scholar-who-supported-uighur-colleague-is-denied-entry-to-china.html

[19] http://www.sampsoniaway.org/interviews/2014/01/07/if-i%E2%80%99m-not-speaking-that-means-im-dead-an-interview-with-liao-yiwu/

concern to left-leaning professors, who predominate in American universities.

5. For many U.S. faculty members of Chinese origin, exchanges between institutions in the U.S. and their home countries represent research and intercultural opportunities that could not be dreamed of just a short time ago. These faculty members serve as important informal ambassadors who create valuable linkages between U.S. and Chinese universities and they should be commended for this. Some faculty members, however, might be more hesitant to criticize China in order to protect these new opportunities, to protect their access to China, and, especially, *to protect family members who remain there.* [20] In some cases, they may articulate, intentionally or unintentionally, positions that mirror official views of the Chinese government and the CCP, and as a result serve, intentionally or unintentionally, as proxies of or apologists for the soft power strategy of the Chinese government. [21]Assessments of the extent to which this occurs must always be based on careful assessment of evidence, and must never be the product of generalized suspicion of faculty members of Chinese origin.

6. Professors who are subject to evaluation for promotion, tenure and salary increases may avoid discussing sensitive topics about China in their classes out of fear of negative evaluations by Chinese students. It is safe to say that Chinese students coming to study in the U.S. have no direct experience of the Western idea of academic freedom. They might be inclined to see critical or outspoken professors as "troublemakers", as

---

[20] In discussions with Wellesley faculty members, this point regarding family members was stressed to me several times as a key reason why some Chinese faculty members were hesitant to be more vocal about criticisms of the Chinese government.

[21] The process of the Chinese government's propaganda strategy regarding overseas Chinese is extensively documented in James To, "Hand-in-Hand, heart to heart: Thought management and the Overseas Chinese", in Anne-Marie Brady, ed., *China's Thought Management* (London and New York, 2012), pp. 164-182.

they are viewed back home. Chinese students coming to the US at present have been brought up in a post-Tiananmen environment of strict political socialization under the "Great Patriotic Education" campaign. Recent sociological research has shown that Chinese students who come to the US express nationalist sentiments: "the current cohort of overseas Chinese students seems, overall, far less critically inclined, and more self-consciously 'patriotic,' than their 1980s predecessors." [22] In U.S contexts, many Chinese students, understandably, respond defensively to criticisms of Chinese society. [23] It is sociologically inconceivable that the presence of nearly 300,000 Chinese students in American higher educational institutions would not have some discernible effects on discussions of sensitive topics related to China.

7. Professors who are publicly critical of particular practices in China, especially those of the CCP, run the risk of being labeled as "anti-China" or "anti-Chinese." This is a common propaganda tactic of the CCP in the face of criticism of its policies and practice, especially with regard to foreign entities. It should always be stressed that criticism of the Chinese government or the CCP is not equitable with "anti-China" or "anti-Chinese" animus. Indeed, the opposite is the case: critical voices, especially those in the Chinese diaspora dissident community, are actively "pro-China" and "pro-Chinese" and criticize the CCP because, in their view, it hurts the Chinese people, thwarts their autonomy, and blocks their path to full realization of their civil and political liberties. The deliberate confusion of critique of specific policies of the CCP with criticism of persons of Chinese or Asian descent is especially effective in the current climate of multiculturalism and identity politics that predominates on American campuses. Accusations of ethnic or racial prejudice or discrimination are particularly effectual tools for silencing dissent and limiting freedom of expression on many different issues. *This tactic is likely to be one of the most effective ones on American*

---

[22] Rowena He, "Identifying with a "rising China"?: Overseas Chinese student nationalism", in Edward Vickers and Krishna Kumar, editors, *Constructing Modern Asian Citizenship* (London and New York: Routledge, 2015), p. 335.
[23] Ibid., p. 336.

campuses for limiting freedom of expression and criticisms of the Chinese government, its authoritarian policies, and propaganda efforts abroad.

What Should Be Done at U.S. Universities?

The fundamental duty of all U.S. universities is the protection of academic freedom as the inalienable moral foundation of the modern university. My concern is that the "default position" that is emerging is one of acceptance of partnerships with Chinese institutions and acceptance of the limitations on and infringements of freedom of speech that these engender. Faculty members whose institutions have partnerships, and who are concerned with the ways in which they might infringe on academic freedom, should be active by:

1. Fostering debates on controversial issues that are avoided on campuses. Since U.S.- China partnerships earmark considerable funds for programming, faculty who wish beyond the boundaries of that programming must be prepared for administrative and collegial resistance and be industrious in seeking out sources of funding for contentious events.

2. Exposing CCP propaganda efforts associated with events carried out in the U.S. under the aegis of partnerships. This task can be enhanced by drawing on the considerable experience and expertise of Chinese dissidents and human rights activists, so as to avoid charges of being "anti-China" or "anti-Chinese". These activists and dissidents should be brought to campuses at every available opportunity.

3. Providing Chinese students with the tools for critical thinking that are the core of the liberal arts, while at the same time understanding and respecting their views and experiences as students who were educated in an environment where independent and critical thinking are highly circumscribed. This is a difficult, but crucial pedagogical challenge and one that is most likely to instill in Chinese students an appreciation for

freedom of thought and conscience that might drive progressive social change in China.

4. Developing courses that deliberately examine controversial topics that are avoided in China and which other faculty in the U.S. environment might not teach in order to avoid "giving offense." These curricular efforts should not be attempts to politicize the curriculum, or present one-sided views, but should endeavor to understand the complexities of controversial issues.

Public Policy Recommendations

Recognizing the threats to freedom of expression that may result from US-China partnerships in higher education is the first step, which this hearing is making possible. Even at this early stage some concrete policy suggestions to political authorities outside of academe who are concerned with the topic of this hearing can be made:

1. There should be an audit of all U.S. institutions of higher education that receive federal funds to establish and document the extent and content of their exchanges with Chinese institutions. Such audits will indicate the precise nature of the relationships between the US and Chinese institutions, with particular attention to how federal funds are being used both in the U.S. and China and indicating any conflicts of interest. In addition, all institutions should provide information on all financial aid and awards taken from official Chinese organizations in the U.S., i.e., Chinese consulates.

2. U.S institutions of higher education that receive federal funds must declare any conflicts of interest that might arise as a result of pursuit of financial gain from the Chinese government. All official ties and activities of U.S. professors or university officers with agencies and apparatuses of the Chinese government and the Communist Party of China should be declared openly, so that actual and potential conflicts of interests of faculty members and officers are open and transparent.

3. All U.S. institutions of higher education that receive federal funds and that have partnerships with the Chinese government must develop real mechanisms and procedures for ensuring academic freedom on American campuses in the course of all formal and informal operations of these partnerships. At U.S. universities, an office, officer, or committee should be charged with making annual audits and reports of all activities that arise from the partnership and making sure that faculty can report irregularities or infringements of academic freedom without fear of retaliation or censure.

———

STATEMENT OF XIA YELIANG, PH.D., VISITING FELLOW, CENTER FOR GLOBAL LIBERTY AND PROSPERITY, CATO INSTITUTE

Mr. XIA. Thank you, to the chairman and the committee.

I have the serious doubt on how the NYU Shanghai campus can possibly avoid the ideological control and the moral education for the students—just for U.S. higher institutions. Because in China we have four—normally we have five courses. That is compulsory courses for undergraduate students, including Marxist theory, Mao Zedong thought. And those courses cannot be avoid.

So I wonder whether the American students—of course, American students, they can choose take this course or not. But the Chinese students, even they are registered by the American universities, they still have the compulsory courses to complete.

So that means that the Chinese students who get degrees from the prestigious universities from U.S., they still have the ideological control and moral education in China. That is one point.

Nowadays, we find in several cases the Chinese authority order to have installed many numerous video cameras for classroom teaching all over in China. So that means that the teachers will be monitored all the time when they give the courses. So, in some cases, the teachers will be talked by either party secretary and some political instructors, say, what you talk about the democracy and the constitutions it is not proper to talk in classroom and so on and so forth.

Nowadays, Chinese regime send a lot of their teachers and set up a lot of their Confucius Institutes overseas. It is a part of the strategy of the grand propaganda overseas. According to the official report, annual report of the 2013, they have established 440 Confucius Institutes and 646 Confucius classrooms in over 120 countries and regions.

We know the expenditure for each Confucius Institute is about half of a million U.S. dollars and, then, that is $60,000 for each classroom. So if you just calculated those total figures, you could see how much they spent on the export of the soft power, actually is the kind of their export of the ideology of Marxism, not socialism.

And as a recent case that American high school students, whose name is called Henry DeGroot from Newton North High School, when he got the opportunity to visit China and exchange ideas with local students, and he choose his ideas on the democracy and freedom. And then, eventually, he was asked to apologize to those students. And the American schools and administrators think he violated rules. That means, American students, you cannot express your own values and ideas in public overseas. That means that you cannot break the taboo. But those kind of taboo, it is the Communist taboo. So that means, the Western people, you have to give up your values and principles while you are traveling overseas.

And in many cases, I think that the faculty members and administrators in the most prestigious universities in the U.S. nowadays, they have some consideration on whether to have the collaboration with China or they persist on their own values.

I know that some universities, they need some more funding and more students come from China. It is a great source for funding. But, meanwhile, they are not challenging the Communist values.

They do not mention the three Ts, Tibet, Taiwan, and Tiananmen, and Falun Gong, and so on and so forth.

And, in my own personal experience at Stanford, as a business scholar, last year, we arranged a talk, speech, used the classroom at Confucius Institute at Stanford. And then we talked about constitutional issues. After that speech, my scheduled speech on the Chinese economy and policies was canceled. And people told me because the people from the Confucius Institutes, they think that your ideas is too aggressive and radical. It is not good. So they will not allow you to give the moral speech in their classroom. But that classroom is located on the campus of Stanford. Doesn't it mean that the occupation of their territory or something in American campuses. So you don't have academic freedom, even on campuses of universities in U.S. So how can you export the liberal ideas to the authoritarian countries if you cannot persist on your own ideas.

And, also, nowadays, the Chinese regime that became very confident after Xi Jinping became the President, they think that they have the free confidence in institutions and theories and, also, in goal. They think that the Communist China will do better than the capitalist countries. So that they have tried to take all alternatives to replace the old values, they think.

For instance, they will say China's model is better than the Western model, American model. They tried to use the Chinese dream to replace the American dream. They use Beijing Consensus to replace the Washington Consensus and so on and so forth. Every thing, every good thing you can find, they will try to find to establish new alternatives. Like Google, they use Baidu, for eBay, they use Alibaba, and for Amazon, they use DangDang. Everything, they will find an equivalent or make alternatives to replace. Like YouTube, they use Youku, and so on and so forth.

So, in the future, that means with expansion, not only the economic expansion, but also military expansion. So China tried to be another superpower and compete with U.S. in many, many things, not only in the economic market activities, but also on values and principles of the human beings. There is a lot of materials to provide with figures and the calculations.

In China, we have so many schools lacking of funding, especially in rural areas. I mean, those poorer students that cannot afford to pay a lot of stuffs for learning. And they cannot get qualified teachers because of the lacking of funding. But, now, China spends huge money to establish Confucius Institutes.

And so what is the point of that? It is kind of the ideological export. It is not international assistance in finance or in some other poverty solutions. I mean, if they really have that money, they should spend in China domestically and in rural areas to lot up their shabby classroom and schoolhouses to be reconstructed or renovated.

So about the NYU campus in Shanghai. They admit that, on this campus, it is hard for you to use Google and others, like YouTube, Facebook, and Twitter. So it is advisable that people should have their own solution, whether use VPN to be paid or they use some other software when they come to China. If they want to get access to all the Internet for academic research, they have to suffer all those inconveniences in China.

So is that the cost and compromise that the universities has to pay? And I have raised that question many times. I said, if there are some dictators were trained, they have their own education in U.S. institutions, can you call that American university as a success for ones to train people in good values?

Like Kim Jong-Un, when he back to North Korea, he became another dictator. So when Bo Guagua, the son of the Bo Xilai, he had all the highest level of education in Britain and U.S. So when he returned, after nothing happened to his dad, it is very possibly for him to become another national leader. So that means more and more dictators will be trained, even in the U.S. universities. So that is a great challenge to our values of education.

I don't know whether there is still time. It didn't show here. So I guess, because of the language barrier, I can only say a few.

Mr. SMITH. Well, Dr. Xia, thank you very much. And I am glad your written testimony is excellent and will inform and help us big time going forward on what to do and what our response should be.

[The prepared statement of Mr. Xia follows:]

Yeliang Xia
Visiting Scholar
Cato Institute
House Committee on Foreign Affairs
December 4, 2014
"Is Academic Freedom Threatened by Chinese Influence on U.S. Universities?"

My Written Statement on the ideological control at home and CCP's penetration in US institutions of higher education with aggressive attitudes of ideological export and comfort of funding and favorable treatment to the American scholars and administrators.

My doubt and consideration is how NYU campus in Shanghai could possibly avoid CCP's ideological control and Marxist education while all Chinese students in the university have to take all these 5 compulsory courses in the first three years of undergraduates and tow compulsory courses for the first year of graduate studies.

It means the Chinese students who will get degrees of Prestigious US universities must meet the requirement for ideological and moral education of CCP while foreign students may choose take those course or alternatives of some Chinese cultural courses by themselves.

In Peking University, there are 5 compulsory courses of ideological political education, 13 credits in total, among which 1 credit is provided by the committee of Communist Youth League in the university with activity arrangement, the rest 12 credits provided by School of Marxism, Peking University through teaching of the courses. These courses includes following:

(1)Elementary Course for Ideological/ Moral Education and Chinese Law (2 hours per week, 2 credits);

(2)Outline of Modern and Contemporary History in China (2 hours per week, 2 credits);

(3)Elementary Principles of Marxism (2 hours per week, 3 credits—2 credits for the course instruction in classroom plus 1 credit for extra-curricular activities);

(4) A General Theory of Mao Zedong Thoughts and Socialist Theory System with Chinese Characteristics (3 hours per week, 3 credits—2 credits for the course instruction in classroom plus 1 credit for extra-curricular activities);

(5)The Current Situation and Policy(2 credits, one per week in average which means two hours classroom instruction every other week, and 1 credit for for extra-curricular activities arranged by the committee of Communist Youth League in the university.

http://www.sis.pku.edu.cn/cn/TeachCenter/Undergraduate/Regulations/0000000016/do

Recently a research survey headed by Davide Cantoni published with the title of "Curriculum and ideology" provided some facts about the control and influence over students in China by CCP.

http://www.voxeu.org/article/curriculum-and-ideology

Liu Yunshan, one of the seven top leaders in China, who is in charge of ideological control and propagandainChina (including nationwideTV, newspaper,journals/magazines and publication as well as arts and Literatur—Movie, drama, opera, music, and many more other show business). He ordered that the propaganda and education of the Chinese Dream must be infused into teaching and education in all levels and types of schools and infused into ideological and moral construction as well as ideological and moral education for university students, infused into cultural construction on campus, it must be infused into textbooks, classrooms and brains and minds of all students.

http://www.dw.de/%E5%88%98%E4%BA%91%E5%B1%B1%E8%AE%A9%E6%AF%8F%E4%B8%AA%E5%AD%A6%E7%94%9F%E8%84%91%E4%B8%AD%E6%A4%8D%E5%85%A5%E4%B8%AD%E5%9B%BD%E6%A2%A6/a-16733421

Here is a notice found on webpage of NYU Shanghai Campus:

NYU now uses the Cisco AnyConnect application for its VPN connections. In China the VPN may be required to access university resources like Google Apps for Education from off-campus locations.

To download and configure the NYU VPN, please click on the appropriate link below.

Windows computer, Macintosh computer, Android device, iPhone, iPad

Note: Please use only vpn-ct.shanghai.nyu.edu as the VPN server address if connecting from mainland China. Other server addresses will not work within mainland China. http://shanghai.nyu.edu/it/vpn

There are many evidences to prove that the Chinese regime has been trying to set taboos for US institutions of higher education. Here is an example:

"China Says No Talking Tibet as Confucius Funds U.S. Universities" By Daniel Golden Nov 1, 2011 7:02 PM ET

When a Beijing organization with close ties to China's government offered Stanford University $4 million to host a Confucius Institute on Chinese language and culture and endow a professorship, it attached one caveat: The professor couldn't discuss delicate issues like Tibet.

"They said they didn't want to be embarrassed," said Richard Saller, dean of Stanford's school of humanities and sciences. Stanford refused, citing academic freedom, and Chinese officials backed down, Saller said. The university plans to use the money for a professorship in classical Chinese poetry, far removed from the Tibet dispute.

http://www.bloomberg.com/news/2011-11-01/china-says-no-talking-tibet-as-confucius-funds-u-s-universities.html

I have my personal experience with the Confucius Institute on campus of Stanford University while I was a visiting scholar at FSI and Hoover Institution, Stanford.

In the early February of 2013, a leader of the students' union invited me to give a speech on China's Macro-economy and policy on, I was glad to accept the invitation and prepared my power point presentation while I was also invited as a commentator for a speech on constitutional issues in China by a well-known scholar came from China. The speech was held in a classroom designated to the Confucius Institute on campus of Stanford, and it was very successful with warm applause and many questions and discussion by the audience.

Yet I received a phone call from the organizer a couple of days after the speech, the student told me that my scheduled speech had been cancelled since the Confucius Institute was unhappy about our discussion on constitutional issues in China, there would be no way to use the classroom anymore. Then I asked if we could change a place since the notice had been sent a few weeks ago, and many people intend to participate. The student told me that he and his team got some pressure, so he could not do anything to assist me.

The Chinese regime became super confident nowadays, there is an incident happened overseas, the story goes like following:

Xu Lin, the director-general of Hanban (the common name for the Chinese Ministry of Education's Chinese National Office for Teaching Chinese as a Foreign Language and headquarter of Confucius institutes) demanded to tear out a page in the brochure with introduction of the Chiang Ching-kuo Foundation for International Scholarly Exchange which is a prestigious foundation located in Taiwan.

http://www.chinapost.com.tw/taiwan/china-taiwan-relations/2014/07/29/413535/Chinas-obstruction.htm

http://www.taipeitimes.com/News/taiwan/archives/2014/07/31/2003596335

http://chinadigitaltimes.net/2014/08/netizen-voices-confucius-institutes-lose-face/

The official overall data from Hanban (headquarter of Confucius Institutes) and typical budget for setting up a Confucius Institute:

http://www.hanban.edu.cn/report/pdf/2013.pdf

http://www.hanban.edu.cn/report/pdf/2010_final.pdf

http://oia.gsu.edu/Search/Agreements/ConfuciusImp-A.pdf

According to Confucius Institute Annual Development Report 2013 , the Confucius Institute Headquarters had published The Development Plan of Confucius Institutes (2012-2020). Confucius Institutes around the world had also laid down their own plans and set up the new goals for their future development. Through the concerted and innovative efforts of both Chinese and overseas colleagues, closer collaborations and continuous improvements in teaching quality have been achieved, thereby enhancing the profile and influence of the Confucius Institute. Through the promotion of language and cultural exchanges, we have worked to build a "spiritual high-speed rail" that connects China with people around the world.

Hanban(headquarter of Confucius Institutes) dispatched 14,400 directors, Chinese language teachers and volunteers to 139 countries, an increase of 3,400 from 2012. We also sponsored over 80 Confucius Institutes to set up Head Teacher Position, supported 10 universities in 8 countries in setting up Majors in Teaching Chinese and trained 5,720 local Chinese language teachers. In an effort to build digital resources, the Confucius Institute Digital Library and Confucius Institute Teaching Case Database and Information Database officially went online. The Confucius Institute Digital Library alone has already amassed more than 188,000 kinds of multimedia resources. developed teaching materials, that totalled 147 volumes.

We donated 700,000 books to 1375 institutions in 120 countries. This included the distribution of 410,000 textbooks to Confucius Institutes (Classrooms), which accounts for 65% of all the books donated.

By the end of 2013, we have established 440 Confucius Institutes and 646 Confucius Classrooms in 120 countries and regions. We have 28,670 full-time and part-time teachers and our registered student numbered 850,000. We have also offered around 40,000 Chinese classes of various kinds and have held more than 20,000 cultural events, attracting over 9,200,000 participants.

Expenditures of Confucius Institutes in 2013

1.Start-up funds for Confucius Institutes (Classrooms) --------$11,002,000.

2.Operational funds of Confucius Institutes (Classrooms)----- $88,684,000.

3.Model Confucius Institutes -----$15,352,000.

4.Salaries of Chinese directors, Chinese teachers (and volunteers)----- $105,459,000.

5.Trainings for directors, teachers and volunteers------ $5,516,000.

6.Confucius Institute scholarships----- $33,829,000.

7.Operational funds for Confucius Institute Online------ $7,984,000.

8.Chinese and foreign expert lecture tours, teaching materials exhibition tours and

student performance tours-----$2,067,000.

9.Development and distribution of teaching materials------- $4,980,000.

10.On-site supervision by Chinese and foreign experts------- $1,294,000.

11.Bilingual versions of Confucius Institute----- $2,204,000.

Total = $278,371,000

Besides the above-mentioned expenditure, there are more items of expenditure, yet the exact data is not available at the moment, for instance, Confucius Institute Online is completely upgraded. This new platform has functions such as interaction teaching, video media and digital commerce. The interactivity of WEB2.0 and the concepts of MOOC teaching were realized, with 9 modules including News, Self-Learning, Live Class, Live Tutoring, Culture, Chinese Tests, Worldwide.

The Confucius Institute provides scholarship for many students overseas, here is some information form the website of LSE, Britain:

The Confucius Institute Scholarships program was launched by Hanban(the Confucius Institute Headquarters) to sponsor foreign students, scholars and Chinese language teachers to study Chinese at a range of Chinese universities(so far good for 142 universities in Mainland China. http://www.lse.ac.uk/CIBL/Scholarships/2014-Confucius-Institute-Scholarship.aspx, 2014-2015 Confucius China Studies Plan

In order to foster deep understanding of China and the Chinese culture among young generations from around the world, enable the prosperous growth of China studies, promote the sustainable development of Confucius Institutes, and enhance the friendly relationship between China and the people of other countries, the Confucius Institute Headquarters has set up the "Confucius China Studies Programme". The Programme consists of six subprogrammes in the academic areas of Humanities and Social Sciences.

The grants are available for the following areas:Joint Ph.D. Fellowship;Ph.D. in China Fellowship;

"Understanding China" Fellowship;Young Leaders Fellowship;Grants for running international conference;Publication Grant. http://www.lse.ac.uk/CIBL/Scholarships/Fellowships-for-PhD-Program---China-Study-Plan-(CSP).aspx

Mr. SMITH. Dr. Richardson.

STATEMENT OF SOPHIE RICHARDSON, PH.D., CHINA DIRECTOR, HUMAN RIGHTS WATCH

Ms. RICHARDSON. Chairman Smith, Congressman Meadows, it is great to see you. Thanks for inviting me to join you.

We have only just begun research in earnest on this topic in the last couple of months. And we consider academic freedom to be a critical form of the freedom of expression. And at a time when exchanges between China and the U.S. and others are increasing, possibly, at an all-time high—and that is a trend that generally we encourage because we think there are enormous benefits in both directions. So we don't do this research because we want to shut these exchanges down. Quite the reverse. We want to make sure that they are taking place within a context of and ensuring the highest standards of academic freedom.

So I think what I can do best this afternoon is just give you some of our preliminary observations based on the roughly 2 dozen interviews that we have done so far. There are two things that every single academic we have talked to has said to us. One is that they are all deeply concerned about this problem.

The other is—and I am not making it up. Literally every single person, at some point in the conversation has said to us, "follow the money." And by that, they have meant everything from who is funding which programs, what quid pro quos exist, what opportunities may be on offer in the future. I have never heard this phrase used so frequently. After somebody said it in the fourth or fifth interview, I thought there is definitely a trend here that we all need to be following.

I think, while the degree of concern about lowering academic expression standards is fairly consistent, I think the individual perceptions of vulnerability, either at an institutional or an individual level, thus far, seems to vary enormously depending on the prominence, the wealth, and the depth of China programs for the institutions or the individual academic in question.

Almost everyone worries specifically about access to China, but the people who continue to be particularly vulnerable, perhaps present—some present company excluded, are young, untenured faculty members who must be able to do field work in order to be able to complete book projects to bid for tenure. I think this is arguably one of the biggest problems to wrestle with.

And, certainly, Americans teaching both in China and outside China have told us quite explicitly that they have chosen to avoid topics such as Tibet or Tiananmen in their classrooms, even when they haven't specifically been asked to do so. Several have also suggested to us, people who have been working on or in China for years, that they feel the pressures have gotten more acute in the last year. That is a little bit harder to nail down specifically.

But the kinds of abuses at the moment that, I think, concern us the most—and stay tuned since we may learn different things over the coming months—is certainly the idea that a far lower standard of academic freedom could become the norm or could become accepted—hi, Mr. Wolf—even when it is clearly stipulated by international law and certainly by practice outside of China. And I par-

41

ticularly want to echo Professor Link's point that there are real consequences for knowledge and not just knowledge of a kind that is important to the academic community, but that is essential, I think, for policy purposes, for economic purposes, for strategic purposes.

The most pervasive kind of problem we have documented so far certainly is about censorship, which seems to come in two different forms. There is self-imposed, which, again, is largely about maintaining access. But there is also imposed censorship, people specifically being told or departments deciding not to focus on certain topics. Again, it is early days to give a definitive view about this, but some of the sensitivity seems to be worse on issues that have an economic or a security dimension to them.

Arguably most alarming to us is the phenomenon of threats to or harassment of students, faculty members, institutions as a whole. We were very alarmed, in an interview just a few weeks ago, when a very senior, very well regarded scholar who is of ethnic Chinese descent said I absolutely change what I say in public because I am worried about the consequences for my family inside China. You know, that is not the world we should be living in.

It is early days to give you recommendations. We usually wait until we are a little further down the track. But I can see offering up to institutions, in particular, a sort of academic freedom safeguards checklist, a bit akin to what businesses or international financial institutions use to assess risk when they are entering into new countries, new partnerships, or new kinds of ventures.

I think it might also be helpful for universities to have to share amongst themselves almost a code of conduct or an action plan where they have agreed, in advance, how they will push back against certain kinds of threats to academic freedom. Many of these different universities are describing to us the same kinds of problems. And I think if there was a little bit more of sharing of those experiences and a commitment to a particular kind of reaction, that protected a higher standard of academic freedom, we might see a lessening of certain kinds of pressure. I think there is probably a long conversation to be had about U.S. Government funded academic exchanges and making sure that rights are protected therein. Perhaps we can save that for the next hearing. Thanks.

Mr. SMITH. Dr. Richardson, thank you so very much.

[Ms. Richardson did not submit a prepared statement.]

Mr. SMITH. And we are joined by Chairman Frank Wolf. Thank you, Chairman.

Just to begin the questioning, and then I will yield to my two distinguished colleagues. Let me just ask you all, you know, New York University was the first with a satellite campus partnership in Shanghai in 2013, Duke, Kean in New Jersey, University of Pittsburgh, Johns Hopkins, Fort Hays in Kansas, Carnegie Mellon, Missouri State University, and University of Michigan have all opened in the last year these satellite, money-rich efforts. And then there are 97 Confucius Institutes in the U.S., 429, as far as we can tell, worldwide operating in universities, in 115 countries. This is an all-out effort by the Chinese Government.

And let me just ask you, if I could, you know, maybe to briefly focus on Hanban and their role in all of this. We understand that some 10,000 teachers are taught every year, recruited and then taught and then deployed. For example, is NYU branding authoritarianism and dictatorship?

We asked the Congressional Research Service to look into this and last year—again, I have asked NYU to be here. I said 15. It was 16 separate dates that we gave them, beginning on February 4th of last year and gave them—we said, ''We are available. We want to hear. We want real answers to genuine questions.'' And they gave us no response or ''can't testify,'' ''scheduling conflicts,'' ''overcommitted,'' and we will continue to try to get them to come here.

But I am especially concerned when the Congressional Research Service finds that for Chinese students—this is at their Shanghai campus—two-thirds of the $45,000 tuition cost is paid for by the Shanghai City Government. That is a huge subsidization, not just of the building that is being handed over, but also to the actual student tuition.

It raises questions. Who, then, gets to be the students? Who controls the admission policies? Maybe you can speak to that. I doubt if it is the son or daughter of a dissident or of, like, Falun Gong practitioner or a Protestant underground church leader or a Catholic Church member who is not a member of the Patriotic Church. It raises serious questions about how—the filtering of who, then, comes in.

You, Dr. Xia, gave excellent testimony about the Marxist mandatory political education, five compulsory courses, Mao Zedong, Marxism, elementary principles. Maybe you could expand on that very briefly.

A good news story is that a number of universities like Chicago and Pennsylvania State have cut ties with the Confucius Institutes. So there are some push backs. I would respectfully say it is happening because of your work. Like, you, Dr. Cushman, the faculty are speaking up and it is becoming a game changer out there. Is that a trend or are these just isolated incidents that are happening? And I have a lot of other questions, but I will just conclude with the other ones and yield to my colleagues.

Last year, the Chinese Communist Party issued the seven noes policy to universities and professors, including no discussion of democracy, freedom of the press, civil society, human rights, the Communist Party's mistakes in the past, the rich and the powerful class, an independent judiciary. How does this apply to the satellites? Do they have to follow that?

And I could just add my own. On the Internet, you mentioned, Dr. Xia, some of the problems there. You know, are they getting the same censorship? In 2006, I held the beginning of a series of hearings on Google. We had Google, Microsoft, Yahoo, and Cisco testify. They were sworn in, and they basically told us they were just following Chinese law in the censorship. Now that has been handed over to Chinese companies who, I believe, are probably even more egregious in their censorship. What happens on these campuses? The Shanghai campus of NYU?

43

Then the last question would be on the enforcement of the egregious, horrific anti-woman policy called the one-child-per-couple policy and forced abortion. No unwed mother in China can have a baby that can't get a birth-allowed certificate. It just can't happen. Now, many women who attend college are still single. How does the college, how does NYU's Shanghai campus, or any of these others implement that?

If you could.

Mr. LINK. I would like to note the presence of Representative Wolf and thank him for coming. He, too, has been stalwart over the years in this cause and that is wonderful. There are a number of questions here. I will just tic off a few answers and turn to our fellow panelists.

On the satellite campuses in China, fundamentally, the self-censorship problem, I think, is the same as the pressures that come to this side of the ocean. And, in my view, those self-censorship problems are still the most far-reaching because they are invisible. You can't see that someone has self-censored. It just happens that the Dalai Lama isn't mentioned and the Tiananmen massacre isn't mentioned and so on.

On the question of the Hanban and the teachers, the Hanban is presented as part of the Ministry of Education. That is false. It is from the State Council. It is from the Communist Party. It is a political program. For those of you who don't know Chinese, Hanban is the name of the office that sponsors the Confucius Institutes and much of this whole global-reach, soft-power project.

The point I would like to make about the teachers in the Hanban is that they are trained to represent the Communist Party when they come abroad and do, so that even in informal contexts when they come to Texas or California or wherever it is, they are—they feel they need to be "patriotic," which means pro Communist Party.

But in their defense, they don't necessarily themselves feel that way. If they are sent abroad and paid by the Hanban in order to be missionaries for the Communist Party of China and don't do it correctly, they can be punished when they go back to China. So it doesn't follow from the fact that every Hanban teacher that comes over is censoring and self-censoring that that is really what is inside them. I think this point we always have to bear in mind—real Chinese people, they are like Dr. Xia—they are real Chinese people, and they have values that aren't that different from our values. Those universal values, I am sorry, is not a myth. It is a true thing.

On the question of the student subsidies that you raised—the access, who gets to go to Shanghai satellite campuses or other campuses—you are quite right to suspect—this is very complex if you go into the statistics of it—but right to suspect that the privileged ones get the best access.

I loved Dr. Xia's point a moment ago when he pointed out how much money the Hanban spends all around the world and neglects the poor children in the rural areas in their own country. This morning, my friend Renee Xia, who is here today—and I talked with Chen Guangcheng, the lawyer, we went to visit him—and that was his point. He knew I was coming to this hearing, and he said, "You have to make it clear that ordinary people in China suffer,

44

and they are not part of this. This is part of a Communist Party elite who is running this program.'' And we mustn't forget that.

I, of course, can't go to China, so I haven't been to the NYU campus. But I will comment that I have a friend who is there—I won't name him because I don't want to do it without his permission—an American scholar. And it answers your question, Mr. Chairman, about whether those rules about ''you must be Marxist and the seven noes and so on'' apply to American teachers who are there. It doesn't to him. He writes me emails about how much friction he goes through trying to defend liberal expression in a context where it goes against the grain to do that.

So I think it is a messy answer to the question there. It is contentious and, of course, should be contentious, so I salute my friend there.

Mr. CUSHMAN. I can't speak to the role of Hanban, in particular, on those kinds of issues.

I would say that, as many people might know from my written testimony and also from the news, I was part of an effort at Wellesley College to speak on behalf of and to help protect Professor Xia after he was fired. And we drafted a letter—it was me and six other faculty members—that was signed by over 140 faculty members, which I would like to take the occasion publicly in this chamber to thank them for doing that, because they didn't have to do that. And it was a very important thing to have done. And it did get attention from other people at other universities, who wrote and said that we would like to do similar kinds of things.

So what I think is that all efforts to combat what I would consider to be the most troubling aspect, when American universities or colleges start looking like Chinese universities and colleges in terms of what you can speak about, it is an effort of resistance and that professors from places that have satellite campuses, professors that have partnerships of the kind that I was talking about that were forged by MUOs that we don't really know much about, there has to be some collective action at that level in terms of pushing back on their own administrations.

And the problem is with many of these smaller-scale partnerships, which I think are obviously more ubiquitous than the satellite campuses, is that they are very often, in almost all cases, forged by the administrations of the universities or colleges and then just announced to the faculty. And so the issues of faculty governance and whether faculty actually control these are coming up, and that seems to me to be something really important to try to effect.

But I would stress, given that people are following the money, given that there is a very distinct political economy of knowledge going on here that is all driven by politics and money, especially at public institutions, which need more money for programs that have been cut, these kind of efforts, these resistant efforts, whether it be teaching new kinds of courses or bringing in dissidents, you are going against the tide, as it were.

Mr. SMITH. I don't know what your time is, and I do hope you can save it. We will have to take about a 15-minute recess. There are three votes on the floor. The one vote is almost out of time, then we have a 5-minute and then another 5-minute.

So we will reconvene, and I hope you can stay. But I do thank you for your patience.

[Recess.]

Mr. SMITH. The subcommittee will resume its sitting. And, again, I apologize for the delay. Dr. Xia, I think you were next up, and look forward to your answers.

Mr. XIA. I would like to mention a few cases in China nowadays.

Some of the university professors when they talked about constitutions and rule of law and freedom, human rights, and then they were removed from their teaching positions, like Zhang Xuezhong in Shanghai and Chen Hongguo in Xi'an. They are both law professors, and they have been removed. And, eventually, Chen Hongguo quit his job. He knows there is no way to continue his teaching.

And also, nowadays, Liu Yunshan, one of the seven top leaders who is in charge of the ideological control and propaganda, and he gave the instructions that the ''Chinese dream'' should be infused into the teaching and classroom and the brains and minds of students. So it is a demand. It is compulsory. No one will be an exception.

So, in China, all the arts and literature and all those show business was under control of the propaganda department of CCP, so, like, movies, dramas, opera, music, and cartoons even. I know that some of the cartoon painters has been arrested only because they made some cartoons to criticize the Communist Party.

So, I mean, the situation is getting much worse than ever before just after the 2 years that Xi Jinping became the President.

And also I found there is, in some of the best universities in U.S., there is a kind of phenomenon. I don't have very direct evidence, but I can sense it. I mean, some professors and administrators, they visit China and they get special treatments like an honored guest, some privilege. Then, in return, they might accept the corrupt officials' children to be the graduate students in those best universities.

Of course, those students have met the criteria, but still there is some room to do something extra. I mean, maybe among 10 excellent students, they will pick up someone that has a direct relationship with the corrupt officials. They know that is much more beneficial than acceptance of the ordinary people.

So this kind of case, I would say, in the way that the American administrators and the professors, they are halfways the dictatorship, in some way, because they make a lot of their compromise when dealing with those Chinese authorities, either in universities and other institutions. That is my impression. And especially for those east Asian studies departments and institutes, they might be lacking of their funding support, and they need to have more visits and cooperative research with Chinese regime, so they might have that kind of a compromise.

One case is, you know, the RAND Corporation, some senior researchers, they had a very close relationship with the administrator in Central Party School, the vice president. And he visit China for 20 times, and each time was arranged by this guy. Anyplace he visited, it would be arranged beforehand. So he got the impression that the Chinese regime became very successful both in economic performance and in the whole life. So I think that that senior researcher got it wrong, because he just believe in that kind of thing through this official arrangement.

So that is my suspects on the effectiveness of a cooperation and academic research between U.S. and China. Thank you.

Mr. SMITH. Thank you, Dr. Xia.

Dr. Richardson.

Ms. RICHARDSON. I will just add a couple of very quick points.

To the issue of which rules will really prevail on satellite campuses, I think most Western universities will say—and in other instances, for example, in the Middle East or with respect to Yale's campus in Singapore, for example, university officials have said, the same rules will prevail as prevail on home campuses. And I think in principle that is lovely to imagine will be the case. I think much depends on how that actually gets tested and how the universities behave when, for example, you know, somebody on a Western university's campus inside China wants to have a symposium about Tibet or Xinjiang or one of the issues we can reasonably expect will be controversial.

And, you know, one assumes that that is some of universities' worst nightmares, but they can't possibly imagine that is not going to happen, right? And whether they are actually really prepared to deal with that in a breach is not clear to us yet.

On the issue of positive consequences that this debate has generated, I actually think that, especially the discussion about Confucius Institutes and their presence in universities and secondary schools in the U.S. actually has the potential to be a very helpful catalyst about a broader discussion about human rights abuses in China and Chinese Government standards, I think in the same way that, for example, you know, tainted products coming from China mobilizes public opinion here in a way that discussions, for better or for worse, about individual cases, for example, or problematic Chinese Government policies doesn't.

You know, I do think that if one of the net results of these debates is that there is more money, particularly for language programs and for research in a variety of fields, that is a positive outcome, as is the presence of lots of academics and students from China in the U.S. I think that is a very positive consequence.

Mr. SMITH. Thank you.

You know, I have been in Congress 34 years, and I remember in my second term a terrible human rights abuse became known through the work of a guy named Steven Mosher, and that is the one-child, forced-abortion policy. And he was taken very credibly, as he should have been. "60 Minutes" and "Frontline" did a tremendous expose largely built on his work. The Washington Post carried a three-part incisive article by Michael Weisskopf, who was the Beijing bureau chief, and I know Mosher, was one of his sources. He had many, but he was one. And yet Stanford denied him his attempt to become a doctor.

And the Wall Street Journal, if I remember correctly, did a piece called "Stanford Morality" and called on Stanford to revisit their concern about access to China when a human rights abuse has been reported.

So it is a longstanding problem—the reason for mentioning this—but it seems it has gotten exponentially worse in the last 10 years, with the Confucius Institutes and now with more and more of our universities setting up satellite campuses in China.

Is it all about money? I mean, it is hard to understand. You know, we all want to get closer to the Chinese people, but when this is all about a dictatorship that is adversarial in the extreme toward its own people, woe to us if we are enabling that dictatorship through this means.

I thought your statement, Dr. Cushman, about how the last to know are the professors, that the administrators are the ones who bring this about—and I know many college presidents, they are always in the hunt for money. It is a very, very difficult job that they have, and they do need to find sources, but not all sources are licit or ethical.

So maybe you could speak to that a bit. And maybe drill down a little bit more about what Hanban is. You know, for most people, that is a word they have never heard before.

One of the things we do in this subcommittee is that it is all about follow-up and action plans that come out of our hearings. As I mentioned, we are already looking at a GAO study so your recommendations on what we ought to ask the GAO to look for, if you could get it officially for the record or just get it to us, we would deeply appreciate that so we get it right on what we are asking. You are the experts.

And, Dr. Xia, if you could just tell us a little bit what it was like going through your travail. Again, thank you, Dr. Cushman, for rallying to his defense so effectively, and your fellow professors. But what was that like?

And then maybe get to those other issues, as well, if you would.

Mr. XIA. While I was teaching in Peking University, for more than 13 years, only in recent 2 years, 3 years, I found some students, they actually reported what I have said in the classroom to the authorities. They think there are some offensive words that go against the party and the socialism. So the authority would think that that would not be accepted since you are teaching university.

All universities in China are all state-owned. It is not private. Even the private universities, actually, they don't have the qualified teachers or sufficient resources to provide qualified education. So in Peking University and Tsinghua and all those universities, you have to obey the CCP's rules.

So people, nowadays, call all the universities in China as the party schools. They are all party schools. So they should be obey the doctrines. Actually, there is no academic freedom. If you say capitalism is might be a good institution, at least in the sense of the research, and people say, no, politically you are not right, so you cannot do that research.

So I know the funding for all humanities and social sciences in China, it all comes from one organization. This organization called the National Planning Committee for Humanities and Social Sciences. It is under the direct leadership of the propaganda department of the CCP. Actually, the office is located in the department of propaganda of the CCP. So that means they are ideologically controlled by CCP. There is no freedom at all to have the academic research.

And so when they have the cooperation with Western scholars, there are also some requirements that says any research that violates the socialist rules and cannot be accepted and cannot be published in China. So they have some warnings to American professors, better not to touch this kind of issue, like Tibet and so on and so forth. Otherwise, this kind of research cannot get funding.

That is the basic situation.

Mr. SMITH. Thank you.

Mr. XIA. Thank you.

Mr. SMITH. If nobody else wants to respond, just a couple of other final questions and anything else you would like to say as we conclude.

At that 2006 hearing that I had with Google, Microsoft, Cisco, and Yahoo, we actually put up on a large board the Google search engine for China. And we typed in a whole lot of things, from ''Tibet'' to the ''Dalai Lama,'' especially ''Tiananmen Square.'' We got beautiful pictures of Tiananmen Square and happy people, but no tanks, no soldiers, no bleeding students. And then when you did Google, the search engine that was available here in the United States, it was millions of hits of what truly happened during those momentous times when so many people sacrificed for democracy and freedom.

What happens on the campuses, like on Tiananmen? What would NYU-Shanghai or any of these in China, these satellites, if somebody says, what happened in Tiananmen Square, what does a professor do? If he is videotaped, is he self-censoring so he is not pulled off and taken by the secret police? I mean, what happens on a day-to-day basis? Because students will always have inquiring minds. At least I hope they will.

What happens?

Mr. LINK. Students, yes, have inquiring minds. And people in China who want to jump over the great firewall and get access can usually do that by using VPNs. It takes work, and you have to play cat-and-mouse with the censors. The problem is that most people are either afraid to do that or don't have the time to do that or just don't think of doing that, so we have, as you correctly point out, this huge inequality of what is available inside China and what is available outside.

I would like to expand a little bit, based on a conversation we had during the break, about this access inequality problem. Chinese students and scholars, including representatives of the Communist Party of China, come to our free society and look at our Googles and our libraries and our free expression and have full access to that, whereas Americans who go to China, along with all the Chinese people, have to jump over these firewalls and figure out how to get what they ought to have had without that struggle.

I want to put this in the context of the problem of censoring books. It has become a controversy in my field of China studies recently whether you should accept censorship of your book about China in order to get it translated and published inside China. Some people say, yes, I will accept the censorship because the larger good is that the rest of the book itself gets through to Chinese readers. And some people say, no, censorship is wrong, and even if it means my book won't get over to the Chinese readers, I am, on principle, not going to do it.

I respect people on both sides of that divide. It is a tough dilemma. But the point is that, at bottom, that is also an access problem. If you think about it, what the Chinese Communist Party is saying to the American scholars is, yes, you can have access to our people to read your book, but the price you pay is that you have to censor what we don't like. So it is fundamentally an access problem.

And I just wonder—I am not a politician—but I wonder if our Government couldn't do something to say that access has to be fair on both sides. If you can have full access to our society, our scholars, our Voice of America, our Radio Free Asia, and so on, we have to have full access to yours. They won't like that, of course, but that is in principle a good argument to have to make.

The final comment I would like to make is about our chairman's observation that in his 34 years of service things have gotten demonstrably worse. I think that is a direct quote, but something like that. You are right; it is demonstrably worse. And in the last 2 years, it is seriously demonstrably worse.

I worry that our society has what I would call a "warning fatigue" about China, because people like Sophie Richardson and Chairman Smith and me and so on have been harping on human rights for 2 decades, and the society might nod their heads, "Yeah, yeah, it is them again, they are doing their thing again," and we are doing our thing again. But somehow we have to get the point across that in these last 2 years it is worse—seriously worse, threateningly worse.

And I will stop there. Thanks.

Mr. CUSHMAN. I would just reiterate the asymmetry problem, the problem in the soft power strategy of China has an open society to work in and we have a closed society to work in. And, you know, the more general problem of open societies is that they have to allow criticisms of themselves, whereas closed societies don't have to allow any of that and they don't.

I did want to say something about the issue of revenue and money, because you are absolutely right. Any college president or provost or someone in charge has to worry about money and sources of money. But my argument has only ever been that, yes, that would be your job. If I were a college president, I would want to maximize the return to my university or my college. But you have to do both. You have to also protect the free space from infringements, subtle and not so subtle.

The subtle ones are more a concern to me, these small acts of self-censorship that continually add up into something much greater. And I am concerned, in terms of "demonstrably worse," what I am concerned about is if our institutions in the United States become more similar to their counterparts in China with regard to what we can talk about not just in China but about a whole range of issues.

I would point out that a colleague of mine, who has actually testified in a hearing before on other issues, particularly related to Tiananmen, who has just published a book on Tiananmen, has had to suffer extreme abuse mostly from, kind of, cyber bullying attacks from all over the place about her views and, you know, personal abuse and ad hominem attacks by orchestrated, kind of, campaigns to criticize her for writing an honest and truthful book about Tiananmen, in which her whole life has been involved in doing.

And this is to be expected in these kinds of cyber attacks that have no origin and you don't know where they are coming from, and they appear to be Chinese people that are attacking her for being anti-China or agents of America or whatever. But lately what has concerned me is when people present critical or provocative perspectives on China and are actually attacked by their colleagues, who are not necessarily of Chinese origin or have Chinese interests, for being too negative about China or not stressing the positive aspects of China.

And when American or, in this case—this talk that I am referring to took place in Europe—when a European professor, you know, really launches an assault on a professor who is telling the truth about China, that starts to worry me. That is only one case, obviously, but I believe that what I am worried about is that that might get worse, that people like us, dissidents or people like Professor Link who speak out, or Dr. Richardson, will be objects of attack for stressing the negative aspects of China and in some ways kind of raining on the parade, as it were, raining on the soft power parade, if I might be indulged with that one.

Ms. RICHARDSON. I think the only point I will add to this at the moment—it seems appropriate when we are talking about academic freedom in China. For anybody who is harboring any illusions about how much space there is on Chinese campuses, I think we would do well to remember not only Ilham Tohti, who has been given a life sentence for essentially trying to have a vigorous, critical conversation in his classrooms about inter-ethnic dialogue, but whose students are being prosecuted, as well. And it is not clear what the outcome for them will be.

But I think that is a pretty sobering reminder of what you can and can't say in a classroom in the mainland.

Mr. SMITH. Dr. Richardson, has the Obama administration shown an interest in pushing back?

You and I have talked many times. I mean, we had a hearing, I will say to our other distinguished colleagues, friends, witnesses, where we had five daughters, all of whose dads were being held, including the daughter of Gao Zhisheng. And when we tried to get a meeting with President Obama with the five daughters, we were told he didn't have the time. He might not agree with the strategy on how do you promote human rights, but not to meet with five daughters that want to say, "Please intervene on behalf of our dads who are being tortured."

I raise this because there has been a tone-deafness on so many of these issues, and I wondering if we are running into the same thing here, that somehow some good will come out of this, when I think it is a gross enabling of bad behaviors and dictatorship. And as I think several of you have said—you have said it, Dr. Link—you know, Xi Jinping in the last 2 years is truly projecting power.

I have had hearings here—because I host part of this sub-committee, the first name of it is ''Africa, Global Health, Global Human Rights''—on the undue influence, the pernicious influence that China is having on African governments—the bad governance model. And they are very close, obviously, to people like Bashir and Mugabe and others. And yet they are starting these institutes in Africa, as well.

Are they concerned about it?

Ms. RICHARDSON. What is the best way to answer this question? The President——

Mr. SMITH. As always, truthfully. As you do. As you do.

Ms. RICHARDSON. I am just trying to find out how blunt to be.

The President did speak publicly at a somewhat abstract level. There were some specifics about Hong Kong, for example, when he was in Beijing. It is our understanding that a more specific discussion was had behind closed doors.

I think the administration is to be commended for the real surround-sound response when Professor Tohti's sentence was announced. There was a White House statement, there was a State Department statement, the President spoke, Secretary Kerry spoke.

But we were very disappointed that not only did the President not follow through on the recommendation that we and eight other organizations made to call publicly for the release of five specific people, including Liu Xiaobo and Liu Xia, but also the President gave an interview to Xinhua, and there is some language in that interview, particularly about ETIM and about terrorism issues, that we find extremely problematic. Because the way it is formulated, I think, very much plays into a Chinese Government narrative about terrorism and about Xinjiang.

And, you know, I don't mean to suggest that there aren't people committing unconscionable acts of violence in Xinjiang. That is clearly happening. I think it is absolutely incumbent on the administration to make a very clear difference between what it knows about specific groups of people who are committing or who are contemplating committing acts of terrorism and the population as a whole.

You know, the latter part of the equation about the relationship between human rights denials and violence or terrorism did get made but, again, in a very abstracted fashion that in no way called the Chinese Government onto the carpet for its abuses in Xinjiang. And I think that is extremely problematic, especially given the priority that the Chinese Government is now placing on terrorism and counterterrorism cooperation with other governments.

So that is a long answer. But, you know, the administration has occasionally been vocal at senior-most levels on specific cases. It has been much less frequent——

Mr. SMITH. Have they shown a concern about the Confucius Institutes and the satellites as to what this really is all about?

Ms. RICHARDSON. You know, I am going to come back to you on that because I haven't looked nearly as clearly as I should have on U.S. Government responses to these issues. I certainly know it is of concern to people.

And I do want to note that there are many people at the working level in the State Department who are pretty ferocious defenders of human rights——

Mr. SMITH. Right.

Ms. RICHARDSON [continuing]. And who——

Mr. SMITH. Well, you know, Dr. Perry made an excellent recommendation about the visas, withholding visas.

In the year 2000, I got a bill passed, the Admiral James W. Nance and Meg Donovan Foreign Relations Authorization Act. One of those provisions has a visa ban for anybody who is complicit in coercive population control and these abuses against women. Less than 30 people have been singled out, and there has been no effort. We get no good answers as to why.

I am all for visas and, matter of fact, correspondingly, or similarly, I wrote the law called the Belarus Democracy Act. Because it is a lot easier for us to criticize Belarus, Lukashenka, there are 200 people on that list, or more, and less than 30 that have been so sanctioned in China.

I think your idea is excellent, Dr. Link, so we will pursue that.

All your ideas are great, and we will, you know, merge them in and merge/purge and go forward with them. So thank you.

Anybody else want to add anything before we close?

You have been great with your time, even greater with your expertise and insights and your leadership.

You know, in Proverbs 22:1, it says, "A good name is more desirable than great riches." I would hope that our universities and colleges who enjoy tremendous names and earned prestige would look at what they are doing in terms of enabling dictatorship, look at the terms and conditions as never before, and, like the University of Chicago and perhaps some others, will sever a relationship that not only enables bad behaviors but also preserves their brand and their good name.

And we will reinvite, as we have done 16 times, NYU to be at this witness table. And this is the first of what will be about a half-dozen hearings going into next year. So you have kicked off I think a very important set of scrutiny and focus probe. Thank you so very, very much.

Mr. XIA. Can I just say 1 minute?

Mr. SMITH. Dr. Xia?

Mr. XIA. I notice one phenomenon is that every year hundreds of English books, including some textbooks, have been translated into Chinese and published in China. But, among them, majority of the books has been deleted a lot. For any contents the authority might not like, there are deletes.

So this kind of thing is a violation of the academic freedom. And also it is kind of cheating and frauding, because the Chinese readers, they don't know which part has been deleted.

Giving one example, it is a very famous book. It is called "The History of Modern China." It is written by Xuejun Yeu, a scholar, American professor, basically come from China, but he lived in U.S. for many years, and now he died. This book has been deleted one-third of the parts of the contents. And the whole version published in Hong Kong, but in China the version is only two-thirds left. So something like that.

I mean, I would like to have the U.S. institutions of higher education to have this in mind. Any publications that will be translated in China, they must pay much more attention on that, whether it is important the contents would be deleted or not.

Thank you.

Mr. SMITH. Thank you, Dr. Xia.

The hearing is now adjourned.

[Whereupon, at 3:09 p.m., the subcommittee was adjourned.]

APPENDIX

MATERIAL SUBMITTED FOR THE RECORD

**SUBCOMMITTEE HEARING NOTICE
COMMITTEE ON FOREIGN AFFAIRS**
U.S. HOUSE OF REPRESENTATIVES
WASHINGTON, DC 20515-6128
**Subcommittee on Africa, Global Health, Global Human Rights, and International
Organizations
Christopher H. Smith (R-NJ), Chairman**

December 4, 2014

TO: MEMBERS OF THE COMMITTEE ON FOREIGN AFFAIRS

You are respectfully requested to attend an OPEN hearing of the Committee on Foreign Affairs, to be held by the Subcommittee on Africa, Global Health, Global Human Rights, and International Organizations in Room 2172 of the Rayburn House Office Building (and available live on the Committee website at www.foreignaffairs.house.gov):

DATE: Thursday, December 4, 2014

TIME: 1:00 p.m.

SUBJECT: Is Academic Freedom Threatened by China's Influence on U.S. Universities?

WITNESSES: Perry Link, Ph.D.
Chancellorial Chair for Innovative Teaching
University of California, Riverside

Thomas Cushman, Ph.D.
Deffenbaugh de Hoyos Carlson Chair in the Social Sciences
Wellesley College

Xia Yeliang, Ph.D.
Visiting Fellow
Center for Global Liberty and Prosperity
Cato Institute

Sophie Richardson, Ph.D.
China Director
Human Rights Watch

By Direction of the Chairman

The Committee on Foreign Affairs seeks to make its facilities accessible to persons with disabilities. If you are in need of special accommodations, please call 202/225-5021 at least four business days in advance of the event, whenever practicable. Questions with regard to special accommodations in general (including availability of Committee materials in alternative formats and assistive listening devices) may be directed to the Committee.

COMMITTEE ON FOREIGN AFFAIRS

MINUTES OF SUBCOMMITTEE ON *Africa, Global Health, Global Human Rights, and International Organizations* HEARING

Day_ *Thursday*___ Date___ *December 4, 2014*___ Room_ *2172 Rayburn HOB*___

Starting Time ___ *1:05 p.m.*___ Ending Time ___ *3:09 p.m.*___

Recesses __*1*__ (*2:08* to *2:28*) (___to ___) (___to ___) (___to ___) (___to ___) (___to ___)

Presiding Member(s)

Rep. Chris Smith

Check all of the following that apply:

Open Session ☑
Executive (closed) Session ☐
Televised ☑

Electronically Recorded (taped) ☑
Stenographic Record ☑

TITLE OF HEARING:

Is Academic Freedom Threatened by China's Influence on U.S. Universities?

SUBCOMMITTEE MEMBERS PRESENT:

Rep. Mark Meadows

NON-SUBCOMMITTEE MEMBERS PRESENT: *(Mark with an * if they are not members of full committee.)*

Rep. Frank Wolf*

HEARING WITNESSES: Same as meeting notice attached? Yes ☑ No ☐
(If "no", please list below and include title, agency, department, or organization.)

STATEMENTS FOR THE RECORD: *(List any statements submitted for the record.)*

Letter from members of the faculty of New York University, submitted by Rep. Chris Smith

TIME SCHEDULED TO RECONVENE _____
or
TIME ADJOURNED ___ *3:09 p.m.*___

Gregory B. Simpkins
Subcommittee Staff Director

58

September 3, 2013

To Members of the NYU Board of Trustees,

We are writing in the spirit of the Board's recent resolve to improve communications with faculty. As elected officers of the university's AAUP chapter, we are advocates for principles that are commonly recognized by U.S. colleges and universities as the gold standard of academic process. (See http://www.aaup.org/report/1940-statement-principles-academic-freedom-and-tenure).

As NYU-Shanghai is opening its doors, we are obliged to record some grave concerns expressed by our members about the prospects for academic freedom in China and at the new campus. These concerns have been triggered by recent arrests of Chinese academics, the removal from the classroom of a law professor for advocating a functioning constitution in China, and by top-level announcements about constraints--known as the "Seven Silences"-- now placed on academic speech in and outside of classrooms nationwide. The latter refers to broad topic areas that will be forbidden in classrooms in Chinese universities as well as in scholarly, internet, and mass media outlets, all but extinguishing the possibility of a learning environment governed by free inquiry. The press has reported that the American co-administrators of NYU-Shanghai have been given formal assurances that academic freedoms will be protected in classrooms and for our students (although the extent of those protections is not at all clear). However, it is difficult for us to imagine the campus can subsist as a bubble on an information landscape that is so severely constrained. Under such circumstances, self-censorship of instructors and students is certain, even if formal state surveillance can be kept at bay, at least within the confines of the campus.

Many of these concerns arise because, like NYU-Abu Dhabi, the Shanghai initiative was conceived and shaped with minimal faculty consultation and with few faculty concerns about freedoms permitted to enter the discussions. Even now, we have not been given any formal evidence of the kind of agreement signed between our NYU Administration and the Chinese authorities (national, municipal or district). Simple questions, such as whether Chinese students are exempted from the nationally-mandated ideological courses that all Chinese students must take to gain a Ministry of Education degree, have not been clarified. We have learned from press coverage that Chinese students will be forced to fulfill their first summer requirement to serve in military camps, and so we wonder if there are other provisions that treat Chinese and international students unequally. These are all questions and issues that should have and would have been raised had NYU-NY faculty with expertise in China and with longstanding experience of the Chinese education and research environment been part of the conversation about the Shanghai campus from the very beginning of its conceptualization.

As a result of these exclusions and black holes in our communication environment, both the NYU-AD and the NYU-SH campuses are widely viewed by faculty purely as administrative initiatives of John Sexton, rather than organic offshoots of the scholarly community that is the core of New York University. This outcome is unfortunate under any circumstances, but all the more so when the university's reputation, and all its employees, risk being tainted by association with rights violations in authoritarian countries like China and the UAE.

To some degree, the sullying of NYU's name has already occurred, notably after the arrests of pro-democracy Emirati academics. Despite the urging of Human Rights Watch, and the AAUP, along with a hundred of our colleagues, there has been no public expression of concern from the NYU-Abu Dhabi administration. Not surprisingly, this refusal to comment on these flagrant assaults on academic freedom has been widely noted, and put down to fear of jeopardizing NYU's favorable financial arrangements with the Abu Dhabi government. Accepting vast sums of money from foreign governments puts NYU and every scholar affiliated with the University in a morally compromising situation, and academic freedom is usually the first casualty.

We fear that a similar pattern will develop in China. The Chen Guancheng affair shows how easy it is for the university's name to get entangled in a human rights imbroglio. Again, the public perception, accurate or otherwise, is that the NYU administration has made commitments in order to operate in China that cannot be imperiled. If that is the case, it is better to know about them now. As faculty, we are in the dark about such matters, though we trust that you are cognizant of them.

Academic freedom is not well-understood, and is often misconstrued by many academics themselves. At root, the protection of academic freedom is not confined to speech in the classroom alone. Like other professionals, faculty have an obligation to share their knowledge and expertise with the public, and it is this extra-curricular interface that is usually most in need of protection. Safeguarding that obligation is the true test of academic freedom and it is why universities cannot operate within a bubble, as they are obliged to do in countries that are hostile to free speech.

We bring these concerns to your attention as a matter of record, and with the open invitation to consult us further on these topics on which the AAUP has almost a century of active engagement.

In our experience, President Sexton has not been attentive to such concerns, and his public comments suggest that he favors a highly selective approach to the protection of academic freedom, invoking it only when it is convenient to do so.

There is a better way to pursue international education, based on initiatives that are guided by faculty interests, faculty expertise, and faculty concerns rather than by administrative fiat. We urge you to advocate for that better way.

Yours respectfully,

Andrew Ross, president, NYU-AAUP
Molly Nolan, vice-president, NYU-AAUP
Marie Monaco, secretary, NYU-AAUP
Anna McCarthy, treasurer, NYU-AAUP
Rebecca Karl, at-large executive member, NYU-AAUP